## Praise for *Manager's Guide to Fostering Innovation and Creativity in Teams . . .*

As an author of books on creative thinking, I read pretty much every book I can on creativity and innovation. As a result I have come to the conclusion that the real voyage of discovery and innovation consists not in seeking new landscapes but in having new eyes for the old one. Charlie's book will have you looking at what you have with new eyes.
> —Michael Michalko
> author, *Thinkertoys,*
> *ThinkPak,* and *Cracking Creativity*

This is a timely, important, and practical book filled with insight and examples and written by someone who has a solid understanding of creativity and innovation. Charlie Prather is a seasoned innovation professional who knows firsthand the challenges of managing for innovation. His experience is unparalleled, and his ability to help those who lead and manage organizations meet the innovation challenge comes at a perfect time. This book is destined to become a well used handbook for all managers.
> —Dr. Scott G. Isaksen, president
> The Creative Problem Solving Group

Charlie Prather's brilliance is teaching creativity and innovation *as a system with functional processes* rather than just giving you the creative techniques needed to run a brainstorming session. His focus on the dimensions and the importance of the human element in innovation brings new light to help you foster innovation on your team.
> —Charles "Chic" Thompson
> author, *What a Great Idea!*
> Fellow, University of Virginia
> Darden Business School

Chapters 10 and 11 on Setting the Environment for Innovation and Leading Innovation treat the subject in profound depth. They, along with all the other chapters, are packed with a huge amount of knowledge, research, and personal experiences that will be valuable to everyone interested in implementing creativity and innovation in their organizations. Based on these two chapters alone, this book is destined to be a classic in the field.

—Dr. David Tanner
author, *Total Creativity in Business and Industry* and *Igniting Innovation Through the Power of Creative Thinking*

# Manager's Guide to Fostering Innovation and Creativity in Teams

## Other titles in the Briefcase Books series include:

To learn more about titles in the Briefcase Books series go to
**www.briefcasebooks.com**

A Briefcase Book

# Manager's Guide to Fostering Innovation and Creativity in Teams

## Charles Prather

McGraw Hill

New York   Chicago   San Francisco   Lisbon
London   Madrid   Mexico City   Milan   New Delhi
San Juan   Seoul   Singapore   Sydney   Toronto

1 2 3 4 5 6 7 8 9 0 DOC/DOC 0 1 0 9

ISBN: 978-0-07-162797-9
MHID:     0-07-162797-9

This is a CWL Publishing Enterprises book developed for McGraw-Hill by CWL Publishing Enterprises, Inc., Madison, Wisconsin, www.cwlpub.com.

McGraw-Hill books are available at special quantity discounts to use as premiums and sales promotions, or for use in corporate training programs. To contact a representative please e-mail us at bulksales@mcgraw-hill.com.

# Contents

# Preface

Today innovation has become our last competitive advantage in the world. As Werner Wenning, Chairman of the Board of Management of Bayer AG, stated at the company's Perspective on Innovation 2008 press forum, "The task is now to set the right course. Only through innovation can our company generate the growth that is essential to safeguard its sustained success."

When it comes to innovation, leaders cannot know enough or be smart enough to even know what to ask for. That's why the collective wisdom of a great team is a critical element in innovation.

Innovation is a social process requiring an effective team to bring a good idea to fruition in the marketplace. This book will help you understand how to build a strong innovation team.

It all begins with the leader and his or her understanding about how to foster a climate of creativity and innovation. I am a firm believer that you don't build teamwork by working on teamwork, because teamwork simulations give simulated teamwork. Rather, nothing builds teams more effectively than working on real problems together, taking risks and creating vulnerability-based trust among team members as new products or new processes are brought to the marketplace. The team leader's ability to establish a climate for innovation is key to building a strong innovative team. In this book you will learn the dimensions of climate and how you can start building it within your team.

# Overview of the Book

The first four chapters cover innovative competence and the basics of innovation and creative thinking—what helps and what hinders. You will learn the overriding importance of the human factors at play in innovation and how to go about creating the working climate that gets people to want to be more innovative. Some high-talent technical people have referred to these skills as "soft skills," inferring that they are unimportant in comparison with the "hard skills" of technology. In reality, those "soft skills" turn out to be the hardest for some leaders to understand and master, whereas the hard skills of technology turn out to be the easiest.

Creativity and innovation need to be thought of as a system rather than as a one-shot deal. When components of the system are in place and working well, innovation will become the normal way you go about the business of leading your team. You will find as you read this book that there are a number of recurring themes that are intertwined. Chief among them are the human issues that more often than not determine the success or failure of any innovation effort. The human issues include the dimensions of the climate for innovation (trust and openness, risk taking, freedom, challenge and involvement, idea time, and idea support being the most important), intrinsic motivation, recognition, and a feeling of being genuinely valued. To foster innovation within your team, you will want to develop a deep understanding of the importance of intrinsic motivation and how to create a climate for innovation that will allow it to flourish.

Before the creation of the DuPont Center for Creativity and Innovation in 1990, it was common practice for leaders to take their teams off-site, usually to a resort location, to develop innovative ideas to solve critical business problems. It was a grand time! People got to know each other better, raised their trust level of each other, played golf, dined in fine restaurants, and occasionally created strategies to solve business problems. However, in looking at the results, we generally got the same kind of ideas that already existed, with a few enhancements, but nothing that we couldn't have gotten by working in the office.

We naïvely thought that getting out of the office and changing our surroundings would cause us to be more innovative. We were wrong. What was missing from these sessions was a structured problem-solving process with effective tools for innovative thinking embedded in it. Process alone is insufficient. Tools alone are insufficient. But together, when skillfully facilitated, they can be dynamite!

In Chapters 5–9 you will learn the system of process and tools that have proved so effective in solving problems innovatively. With practice you will be able to help your team solve critical problems more innovatively while fostering a climate of innovation within your team.

Leaders who foster innovation in their teams must rely on the ideas from the team members. Ideas from your people truly are gifts and you should regard them as such. However, gifts can be refused. How would you feel toward someone who refused a birthday gift you'd carefully selected? I strongly suspect you would never give that person another gift and you would likely feel negatively toward him for a long time.

Chapter 10 discusses implementation planning. After all, innovation and creativity provide competitive advantage only if you take action.

The following chapter outlines the four tasks of leaders of innovation. Leaders today must have the interpersonal skills and know-how to create the conditions at work (the working climate) so that everyone will want to give the gifts of innovative ideas that can result in sustainable competitive advantage for their organization.

When people on your team are in the right jobs, they are happier, produce more, and are less likely to leave. They are also more likely to contribute their gifts of innovative ideas. In Chapter 12 you will learn how to increase the likelihood that people find the jobs that are right for them by matching their style of problem solving to that demanded by the job. You will learn that if smart, capable, and well-meaning people just aren't doing a good job, it is more than likely that they are in the wrong job. What you will learn in Chapter 12 will put you in a position to help them succeed in the right job.

## In Summary

You are obviously interested in fostering a climate of innovation on your team so that business results will be more innovative. You can set the stage for total organizational innovation by beginning with your team. Yours can be a model that other teams might wish to follow. Read on to see how you can lead your team or organization to be more competitive through innovation.

## Special Features

The idea behind the books in the Briefcase Books series is to give you practical information written in a friendly, person-to-person style. The chapters deal with tactical issues and include lots of examples and how-to information. They also feature numerous sidebars designed to give you specific information you can use. Here's a description of the boxes you'll find in this book.

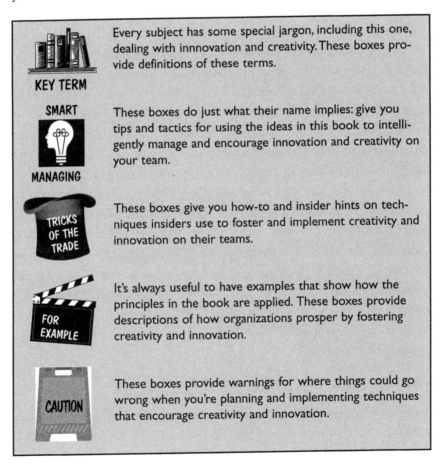

**KEY TERM** Every subject has some special jargon, including this one, dealing with innnovation and creativity. These boxes provide definitions of these terms.

**SMART MANAGING** These boxes do just what their name implies: give you tips and tactics for using the ideas in this book to intelligently manage and encourage innovation and creativity on your team.

**TRICKS OF THE TRADE** These boxes give you how-to and insider hints on techniques insiders use to foster and implement creativity and innovation on their teams.

**FOR EXAMPLE** It's always useful to have examples that show how the principles in the book are applied. These boxes provide descriptions of how organizations prosper by fostering creativity and innovation.

**CAUTION** These boxes provide warnings for where things could go wrong when you're planning and implementing techniques that encourage creativity and innovation.

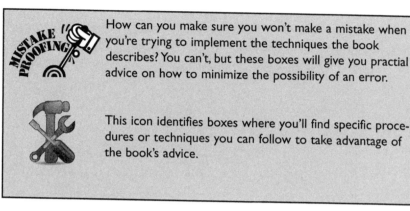

How can you make sure you won't make a mistake when you're trying to implement the techniques the book describes? You can't, but these boxes will give you practial advice on how to minimize the possibility of an error.

This icon identifies boxes where you'll find specific procedures or techniques you can follow to take advantage of the book's advice.

## Acknowledgments

I wish to acknowledge those who contributed importantly to this book. Jack Johnson, my partner and colleague, whose great knowledge, experience, and devotion allowed him to provide invaluable encouragement and assistance in proofreading for content and continuity, and contributed much to making this book helpful, enjoyable, and readable.

Dave Tanner saw in me the possibility to manage the DuPont Center for Creativity and Innovation and generously gave me the opportunity. Cy Hood, my high school chemistry teacher, inspired me to further study and to a happy career in the field. My mother always believed in me through hard times. Richard Tait, my colleague, provided the stories about Apple. Many other contributors freely gave of their time and attention to provide truly inspiring stories of innovation from which we all can learn a great deal.

We all learn from stories, and it is my hope that the stories from real companies and real people will serve as templates that you can use in fostering creativity and innovation in your teams.

# The Innovative Organization

W hen the DuPont Center for Creativity and Innovation was created, we needed a model on which to structure our offerings. Having been a manager of research and development for some 18 years, I drew from my personal experience about the environmental factors that help innovation and the ones that can quash it. Since that time I have refined the model that appears in Figure 1-1. I call it the "Innovation Competence Model," since the model works for most any organizational competence.

## The Three Arenas of Innovation Competence

The three arenas of the competence model are *education* about the principles, tools, and techniques of creativity and innovation; *application* of these principles, tools, and techniques to solve critical business problems; and *leadership* in the workplace to enable innovation. Developing an internal competence for innovation requires a systemic approach in all three arenas.

It is a mistake to think that focus on one area alone will result in an increase in innovation competence. That's why training in creative thinking techniques alone will be uniquely ineffective in improving innovation competence unless there is attention given to the remaining areas, application and leadership. Leaders who delegate innovation to the training department will always be disappointed with the outcome, since innova-

**Innovation** A new way of doing something or a new product or service.

**KEY TERM** Although the term can be applied to anything new, typically there's a distinction made between invention, an idea that becomes a reality, and innovation, an idea that's applied.

"Innovation is new stuff made useful," according to Max McKeown in *The Truth about Innovation* (Pearson Education Limited, 2008). "That's just about the best definition. It clears up what's interesting about innovation without overcomplicating."

tion requires total commitment and leadership from the very top of the organization.

Since I first published this Innovation Competence Model (*Blueprints for Innovation*, New York: American Management Association, 1995), a number of organizations have embraced it, most notably the 3M Company's Grass Roots Innovation Team (GRIT), whose members found they were

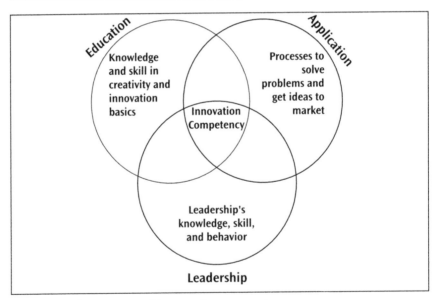

Figure 1-1. Three areas of innovation competence

already doing what the model illustrated. As Kim Johnson, leader of the 3M GRIT. says, "The Model of The Innovative Organization gave structure and brought clarity to what we were doing, and made it easier to communicate to upper levels of leadership. We were happy to have independent confirmation of our programs and activities." If you are to use this book as

---

**SUPPORT AND PROMOTE INNOVATION FROM THE TOP**
Consider the issue of employee safety. In companies where
safety is a strong organizational competence, there are
safety educational activities and meetings on a regular basis, the procedures
for ensuring safety are always applied in the workplace, and most of all top
leaders personally support safety and make it a big part of their personal
performance metrics. That's why safety is a strong internal competence.
What would happen if the top leaders delegated all that to the training
department and took no active part in the safety program themselves? People would not take safety seriously.

The same is true of innovation. The innovative organization supports
innovation at the highest levels with elements in the three areas of education, application, and, most important, leadership.

---

a guide for innovation in your organization, we recommend you use the
Innovation Competence Model as the unifying system for defining and for
describing each specific activity.

At the DuPont Center for Creativity and Innovation, we offered
courses in creative thinking (education) and facilitated problem solving
workshops (application), but we naïvely assumed that leaders in a company known for innovation would themselves know how to lead it. That
was a mistake. Since then we have developed a strong focus on innovation leadership so that innovation can continue after the consultant goes
home. We now know that total leadership commitment from the top is
the single most important factor in a company's level of innovation competence and its innovation success.

## Innovation Leadership from the Top

In the first of several insightful articles on the short life span of some 20
"centers of innovation" in major U.S. corporations—all of which were
discontinued ("Can Corporate Innovation Champions Survive?" *Chemical Innovation*, November 2001, Vol. 31, No. 11, pp. 14-22; available at
*pubs.acs.org*), Jack Hipple points out vividly the absolute requirement
for solid and consistent involvement and commitment from the topmost leadership. In addition he points out that the people who were the
leaders of innovation centers all differed significantly in creativity and
personality style from their superiors, whose continued support was
necessary for survival. The innovation center leaders were tolerant of

ambiguity and strongly preferred the "change the system" problem-solving style (see Chapter 12), whereas the managers to whom they reported were intolerant of ambiguity and preferred the opposite "perfect the system" problem-solving style. This great dissimilarity was not understood at the time and caused real problems in seeing value and in communication. Hipple also points out that many of the physical facilities that were created and decorated with great excitement and fanfare are today computer rooms.

There are three important lessons:

- Topmost leadership support is absolutely vital.
- All parties need to truly value diverse problem-solving styles.
- Physical trappings are relatively unimportant.

In company after company, we have seen innovation delegated to lower-level people, only to falter for lack of support from the top. If you want to understand the true value system of any organization, look at the budgeting process. Which functions get the money. Is there a budget for innovation?

## Apple's iPod and iPhone: Models of Top Management Support

The story of the development of the iPod illustrates the effective and critical role that leadership from the top plays in innovation. Steve Jobs is one of the most iconic and celebrated leaders of innovation in the business world today. Since his return to the leadership of Apple in 1997, the company has been reshaped and has created a continuing stream of high-impact, customer-focused innovations that Jobs was responsible for leading as CEO. Jobs has been so successful at reinvigorating the innovation machine at Apple that it has been recognized by *Business Week* four years in a row (2005-2008) as the world's number-one innovative company.

Nothing epitomizes Apple's resurgence and Jobs's ability to align his organization around a singular and powerful vision more than the iPod. As Jobs said, "If ever there was a product that catalyzed Apple's reason for being, it's this [iPod], because it combines Apple's incredible technology base with Apple's legendary ease of use with Apple's awesome design." When the iPod project was launched in early 2001, there were already portable digital music players on the market, but they were difficult to use and poorly done. Jobs had a vision of transforming the portable music listener's experience so that with the iPod "listening to music will never be the same again."

The first step was aligning the whole organization around the vision of creating a high-capacity music player that could hold the user's complete music library. In

> ### STEVE JOBS
>
> SMART
>
>
>
> MANAGING
>
> Steve Jobs has a reputation of being abrasive, demanding, and often contemptuous of those he doesn't respect. But the one thing on which virtually all unanimously agree is that he is phenomenally effective at inspiring people to do their best work. His commitment to a clear vision, his ability to communicate and share that vision, his skill at aligning everyone on his team around that vision, and his ability to shape the final output to meet that vision have been key elements of his success (John Heilemann, in "Steve Jobs in a Box," *New York Magazine*, June 25, 2007).

addition, in the words of Steve Jobs (quoted in the Apple press release, October 23, 2001), "With iPod, Apple has invented a whole new category of digital music player that lets you put your entire music collection in your pocket and listen to it wherever you go." The iPod changed the way people listed to music forever—and it went from project launch to full commercialization in less than a year, in time to hit the Christmas buying season. The goal of launching such an innovative product in that short a time could have been deemed impossible by the team and created an insurmountable obstacle to getting organization buy-in. But Jobs and his team sensed that while the final *product* would be a radical breakthrough, most of the key product components needed for success were already available.

And today we have the iPhone 3G, again as a result of single-minded devotion and personal commitment from Jobs himself. When it comes to innovation, there is just no substitute for passionate personal commitment from the very top of the organization.

## Innovation Choices During Hard Times

Top leaders with a narrow focus on immediate profits tend to make serious mistakes regarding innovation when trying to cope during periods of serious economic downturn. Innovation is the lifeline to the future; in

## Nothing Succeeds Like Commitment

The results of Jobs' commitment to make the iPod happen have been nothing short of spectacular. The iPod was launched on schedule in October 2001 and quickly became the number-one portable music player on the market, surpassing the Sony Walkman record of 180 million units sold. Jobs led the organization to continuously innovate and expand the product line and enhance its appeal to the point that the iPod and its associated offerings (particularly the i-Tunes Music Store) were generating upwards of 50 percent of Apple's revenues.

fact, innovation helps ensure there will be a future. However, many CEOs trim costs quickly by throwing the lifeline overboard to reduce weight during the storm of poor economic conditions.

Innovative organizations make choices that favor innovation. Less innovative organizations make choices that favor the stock price. The stock price is a tyrannical boss that will squeeze out innovation every time because of its focus on the near term. I have worked with a number of small privately held companies still run by their entrepreneurial founders. They don't worry about next week's Wall Street analysts' meeting; they make business decisions with their grandchildren's future in mind!

One of the best ways to understand the choices being made in your organization is to examine the budget. It is in the budget that the true values of any organization are displayed for all to see. Which programs get the money? All too often company leaders will fund an innovation project with just enough money to keep it running at a low level so that it doesn't quite die.

Some of the worst mistakes that top managers can make in a downturn that will hurt innovation were described by Bruce Nussbaum in *BusinessWeek*, (online January 13, 2008). On the surface these actions seem fair enough, because they will save money in the short term, but at the sacrifice of innovation. I have abstracted them below:

1. **Fire talent.** Talent is too valuable to be treated as an expense. It is our biggest competitive advantage when it comes to innovation.
2. **Cut back on technology, particularly IT.**
3. **Reduce risk.** Risk and innovation go hand in hand. There cannot be innovation without risk. Leaders need to fight the temptation to fund

only surefire ideas guaranteed not to fail, since these are also guaranteed to not be very innovative. Once entrenched, risk aversion becomes a very difficult cultural norm to reverse.

> ### RESOURCED TO WIN
>
>
> I have seen programs resourced with as little as one-tenth of a person—just one day every two weeks! I like to think of that as *resourcing it not to lose,* when in fact a program will bear fruit only if it is *resourced to win.* It's better to have one project fully resourced that has a chance of winning than to have 10 that are underresourced, guaranteeing that none can win. The same amount of money will be spent with either strategy, but with which strategy would you rather be associated?

4. **Stop new product development.** Companies that have their eye on the future continue to develop new products and have new offerings as soon as the market turns around (witness the iPod), beating the pants off companies that did otherwise.

5. **Replace growth-oriented CEOs with cost-cutting CEOs,** who then replace innovation as a key strategy. Cost-cutting CEOs leave innovation behind: they cut costs from existing programs and may neglect to think ahead to what's coming next and where they're going.

Recessions don't last forever. Winning companies usually emerge with something new for the marketplace because they've kept working on it during the downturn. Apple worked on iTunes, iPod, and its retail stores during the last recession and came out winning once growth returned.

## Categories of Innovation: Finance, Process, Offerings, Delivery

Doblin, Inc., an "an innovation strategy firm" (*www.doblin.com*), has categorized innovation into four major categories—Finance, Process, Offerings, and Delivery. Within these categories it has further subdivided innovation into 10 types.

The major point here is that while most people think of innovation in terms of product innovation, there are a great many more business opportunities for innovation that can return greater profits with less work. For example, in the Finance category there is *business model* innovation, such as Dell's made-to-order computer built specially for each customer, with payment in advance. In the category of Delivery, another type of innovation is *customer experience*—how customers feel when they do business with a company. Think about the loyalty that Nordstrom's customers feel (see sidebar) or the special feeling guests experience at a Ritz-Carlton hotel.

In the Process category, Spark Labs LLC of Tampa, Florida has innovated its in-house rapid new product development process, and it's paying off handsomely (see sidebar). Charles Armstrong, CEO, explains that Spark Labs LLC is a new product development machine whose focus is to create new products, brand them, and then sell the brands once they're successful.

Many companies spend small fortunes developing proprietary products and technology and then subsequently patenting them. Spark Labs has reinvented the process to maximize profits and minimize investment.

> **FOR EXAMPLE**
>
> ### THE NORDSTROM WAY
>
> In one of my workshops a participant related the story of going to a Nordstrom store with his wife to buy shoes. One of her feet was a size different from the other, and the wife had been accustomed to buying two pairs and discarding the unused ones. The Nordstrom sales associate gave her the correct sizes, charging only for one pair. The workshop participant said that one event made them Nordstrom customers for life.

1. Solution-centric brainstorming sessions (radical ideas welcome)
2. Adaptation of three to five core concepts to market-feasible products
3. SWOT analysis of market landscape and research via Google Patents
4. Development of one product within a potentially proprietary space
5. Submission of provisional patent applications to the U.S. Patent and Trademark Office
6. Congruent brand development
7. Internal consumer testing following industry-recognized practices
8. Product revisions
9. Trademark filing
10. Brand extension to multiple consumer contact points (on- and offline)

11. Development of engaging, data-driven presentation to highlight the new brand
12. Pitches to various, prospective licensees/buyers for initial reaction
13. Performance of a full patent search, contingent upon licensee/buyer interest
14. Extension of the provisional patent application to full utility patent application (if necessary)
15. Sale of intellectual property and surrounding brand

Here's how Armstrong explains the process for Cord Cuffs:

In 12 months' time, we've taken a 'napkin concept' to market, and done so with very, very little financial investment. Initially, we spent our time researching the market landscape and viable materials for our own cord management solution. Once we'd developed (and filed multiple provisional patent applications for) a design that was cheap to make, yet high quality and effective, we shifted our focus to productization. Name, logo, packaging, Web site . . . everything. With this, we then performed several rounds of consumer testing—each time refining our materials so as to better communicate the product's utility while simultaneously forming an emotional bond with the consumer via branding. Once our messaging was completed, we settled on manufacturing partners and had 10,000 Original and 10,000 Heavy-Duty Cord Cuffs made. We then equipped our national network of 150 sales representatives with both sales presentation materials and physical product samples. From there, our emphasis then moved to support—supporting our reps with everything from training materials and in-use graphics to bulk-pricing and licensing agreements.

**CORD CUFFS**

One of the latest Spark Labs products is Cord Cuffs— clever devices for holding the many electronics cords to your office desktop so they'll stay put. Cord Cuffs is a homegrown innovation, so the company has precisely developed this product line according to the outlined protocol—and the results have been nothing less than remarkable. According to CEO Charles Armstrong, "Cord Cuffs are now being sold in a number of stores, sold online, in one of the nation's largest catalogs (Taylor Gifts, www.TaylorGifts.com), and are being private-labeled by Europe's largest direct selling organization within office supplies."

FOR EXAMPLE

This is an excellent example of the Innovation Competence Model in action. It shows a systematic and supported approach encompassing the three arenas of education, application, and leadership.

Now, let's get into the basics of innovation.

# Manager's Checklist for Chapter 1

☑ Sponsor activities in the education, application, and leadership arenas to foster innovation in your team. Make comparisons to the safety program in your organization as you think about how to systematize innovation.

☑ Always remember that support of innovation by the top managers is absolutely vital for its success. If you're not the topmost leader in your organization, find ways to involve those whose support you need: make them part of your initiative early on (Chapter 2) so that their support will be available for you.

☑ During hard economic times, continue innovation work, so that when better times return, you will be ready to profit. Also adequately resource one good project that has a chance of succeeding rather than inadequately resourcing a large number of projects, which guarantees that all will lose.

☑ As you decide where to spend your innovation dollars, remember to look not only at product innovation, but also at the other types of business innovation. A good place to start is streamlining your process for new product development. Find ways to build customer loyalty for life by providing outstanding service.

# Innovation 101

C reativity and innovation are really all about problem-solving. I like to think of problem solving as the continuum shown in Figure 2-1.

At the center of the continuum, your system is meeting expectations. But if things go wrong, you move to the left where the goal is to solve the problem and return your system to meeting normal expectations in the center. You might think of this kind of problem solving as remedial, fixing what's broken. On the other hand, if your system is meeting expectations but you're dissatisfied with the rate of growth or you feel a need to create a new product or service to be more competitive in the marketplace, you will need to move to the right on the continuum. You might think of this kind of problem solving as innovative, creating what you don't have.

## Use the Right Process for the Problem

The tools and processes that help us fix what's broken are very effective and we all need them every day. These tools include Six Sigma, TQM, and the analytically based problem-solving tools. These tools are effective on the left side of the continuum, fixing what's broken and bringing the system back to normalcy. However, they are not effective at creating what we don't already have.

For this kind of challenge we need a different kind of problem solving, namely, innovative problem solving that helps us create new tech-

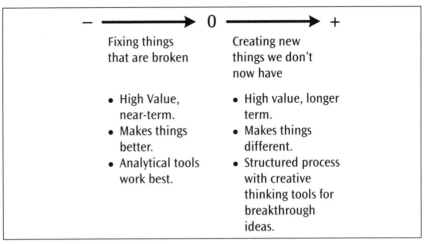

**Figure 2-1.** Types of problem solving—a continuum

nologies, new solutions, and new products and services to delight our customers. Since this book is about innovation, I am referring to innovative problem solving that lies to the right of the continuum of Figure 2-1.

## Innovative Problem Solving

Figure 2-2 illustrates a simplified form of an innovative problem-solving process. The process begins with a problem, a need, or an opportunity. First, we define the problem clearly. Then the process of idea generation occurs, yielding a number of good ideas. The best ideas are selected and the process of implementation yields a result on the right, the desired outcome, whatever it might be, depicted as dollar signs.

Which of these processes is the most important? Obviously, all are equally important, for one without the others is woefully incomplete.

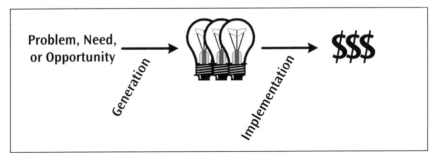

**Figure 2-2.** Idea generation and implementation in problem solving

In Figure 2-3, I have added the "cloud" of working climate above the whole process of problem solving. The dimensions of the working climate will powerfully assist or powerfully impede both the generation and the implementation processes. The dimensions of the working climate for innovation are treated fully in Chapter 10.

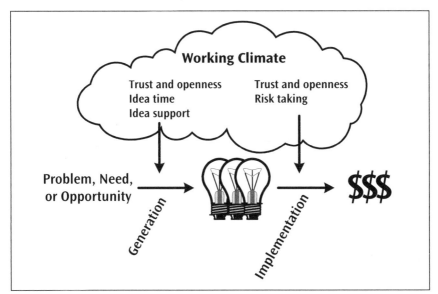

**Figure 2-3.** Influence of working climate on idea generation and idea implementation

It's obvious that the idea-generation process will be assisted by a climate that allows time to generate ideas and provides support. In addition, trust among team members and leaders is crucial. In the same way, the idea-implementation process is assisted by a climate characterized by trust and openness and that also values (or at least tolerates) risk taking.

Naturally, implementation would be impeded by a climate that punishes mistakes. People are often paralyzed by the fear of failure, which makes trying something new exceedingly difficult, if not impossible. For this reason, a working climate that discourages employees from taking risks and instills a fear of failure is always a major barrier to innovation. I'll have a lot more to say about that in the section on the climate for innovation in Chapter 10.

## Role of Divergent and Convergent Thinking

In Figure 2-4 I have added "diverge" and "converge" to signify that divergent thinking is predominantly needed during the idea-generation process and convergent thinking is predominantly needed during the implementation process. During divergent thinking, people create new ideas and build on ideas to enrich the number of choices. During convergent thinking, people use their experience and exercise their judgment to select the best ideas and implement them to deliver a bottom-line result.

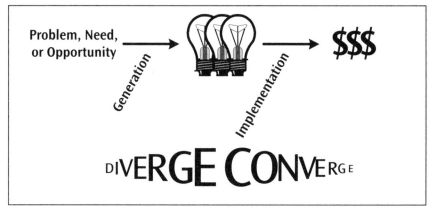

**Figure 2-4.** Divergence and convergence in problem solving

Every adult is strongly conditioned to gravitate toward convergent thinking, primarily because we were educated that way and your organization rewards it—it pays! However, we must use divergent thinking when we need to generate new ideas and we must use convergent thinking when we need to make choices. The challenge is not to contaminate one with the other.

Dr. Scott G. Isaksen (author of *Creative Approaches to*

> **KEY TERM**
>
> **Divergent Thinking** Mental activity that moves in different directions from a common point. Divergent thinking is open and expansive. Divergent thinking seeks to build, amplify, decorate to make something more or different.
>
> **Convergent Thinking** Mental activity that moves toward a single point. Convergent thinking is critical and restrictive. Convergent thinking seeks to select, judge, compare, make things happen, deliver a bottom-line result.

> ## WHEN DIVERGING, BE LESS ADULT
>
> When adults see or hear a new idea, they compare it against **CAUTION** their internal database (or mental filters). If the new idea is consistent with their mental model of what they know to be a good idea, they will label it as good (especially if it was their idea). However, if the new idea is not consistent with what they already believe about that subject, they will likely label it as bad and point out what's wrong with it.
>
> In contrast, children who do not have a large internal database are much more likely to find what's right about a new idea rather than instantly point out what's wrong. Adults start considering any new idea by silently asking the question, "What's wrong with it?" whereas children silently ask a different question, "What's right with it?"

*Problem Solving, Meeting the Innovation Challenge,* and *Toolbox for Creative Problem Solving*) likes to say that divergence is making *lists* and convergence is making *choices.*

It is the contamination of divergent thinking by convergent thinking that leads well-meaning people to instantly judge new ideas. Likewise it is the contamination of convergent thinking by divergent thinking that leads well-meaning people to endlessly

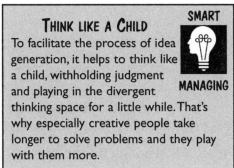

> ## THINK LIKE A CHILD                  **SMART**
>
> To facilitate the process of idea generation, it helps to think like a child, withholding judgment and playing in the divergent **MANAGING** thinking space for a little while. That's why especially creative people take longer to solve problems and they play with them more.

delay implementation because they always want to enrich the idea being implemented.

We've all been in team brainstorming meetings where someone summons the courage to suggest an idea to solve a problem, only to have it quashed by another team member with a comment such as "It won't work," "The boss won't go for it," or "It's not in the budget." These *killer phrases* demonstrate that convergent thinking is alive and well—and hurting divergent thinking.

In our experience, it is the experts—those individuals with great knowledge, experience, and credibility—who are the very first to tell everyone why a new idea will not work. However, it is precisely these

**CREEPING INTO DELAYS** Hewlett-Packard has a term for this behavior of divergent thinking during the implementation process—"feature creep." Engineers might want to delay the commercialization schedule of a specific printer so they can add another function to it. Software developers are particularly susceptible to this contamination problem.

**Killer Phrase** A statement that stifles creativity. It's defined by Chic Thompson, **KEY TERM** author of *What a Great Idea! 2.0* (Sterling Publishing Co, Inc., 2007), as "a knee-jerk response that squelches new ideas; . . . a threat to innovation." The effect of a killer phrase is that it reduces possibilities by putting an end to something from the start.

experts who have the most to contribute to the process of innovation!

## The Five Pitfalls That Hinder Innovation

There are five major pitfalls people and organizations tend to encounter when trying to become more innovative:

- Working on the wrong problem
- Judging ideas too quickly
- Stopping with the first good idea
- Obeying rules that don't exist
- Failing to get sponsorship and build coalitions

Each of these will be described in detail below. As you read, see how many of these apply to you or your organization, so that you can avoid them at every opportunity.

### Pitfall #1: Working on the Wrong Problem

When smart people are given a problem to solve, they almost always instantly jump into it with both feet, creating good ideas to solve the "problem." Unfortunately, many, many times what they take to be the problem is really a litany of symptoms of the problem lying underneath all the clutter.

If you are very sure that you know what the problem is, you can almost be certain that you don't fully understand the situation. And it's not because you're not smart—that's not the point. The point is that the problem usually hides under a set of symptoms that people like to talk about. If you are engaged in customer service work of any type, you already know that customers will almost always give you a list of symptoms rather than a completely and correctly defined problem.

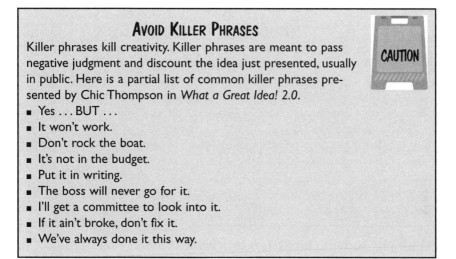

## AVOID KILLER PHRASES

Killer phrases kill creativity. Killer phrases are meant to pass negative judgment and discount the idea just presented, usually in public. Here is a partial list of common killer phrases presented by Chic Thompson in *What a Great Idea! 2.0*.

- Yes ... BUT ...
- It won't work.
- Don't rock the boat.
- It's not in the budget.
- Put it in writing.
- The boss will never go for it.
- I'll get a committee to look into it.
- If it ain't broke, don't fix it.
- We've always done it this way.

CAUTION

Work hard to define what you really want during problem-solving sessions; that is, be sure you have identified the real problem correctly. Of all the pitfalls to be avoided, this one is most important, for you can aggressively bark up the wrong tree and get nothing for your efforts but a lot of noise and an echo.

In our innovative problem-solving process, we use the WIBNI (wouldn't it be nice if . . . ?) approach to help identify the right problem. This is described in detail in Chapter 6.

Once a construction industry company requested my help because they were having trouble with a pesky customer. The request was to help the company learn how to get rid of its pesky customer. We used the WIBNI process to help define the real problem, which turned out to be "How might we convert this adversarial customer into an ally?" It made a lot more sense and was a productive problem-solving session.

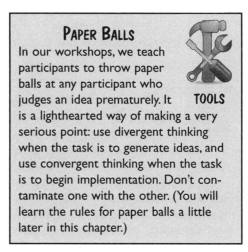

## PAPER BALLS

In our workshops, we teach participants to throw paper balls at any participant who judges an idea prematurely. It is a lighthearted way of making a very serious point: use divergent thinking when the task is to generate ideas, and use convergent thinking when the task is to begin implementation. Don't contaminate one with the other. (You will learn the rules for paper balls a little later in this chapter.)

TOOLS

FOR EXAMPLE

## STAMPING OUT UNNECESSARY COSTS

In the early 1990s a worldwide travel reservations company in Texas was sending invoices to its clients every month, a practice it had been following since its birth a number of years earlier.

However, the postage was being applied inaccurately, resulting in much higher postage costs than necessary for the company.

Several people had worked on this issue for some time. Then someone suggested that the problem was really getting the billing information to the client, rather than applying the right postage. With that view, a very young employee knowledgeable about the fledgling Internet suggested the company begin sending electronic invoices over the Internet. That idea resolved the problem at a significant savings.

## Pitfall #2: Judging Ideas Too Quickly

Most everyone gets paid for convergent thinking most every minute of every day at work. It pays! A convergent mindset creates results and everyone seems to be happy about that. In fact we are so good at convergent thinking that we use that style even in the idea-generation phase of problem solving, when divergent thinking is necessary. That is what causes people to judge ideas too quickly, which is the second pitfall we must learn to avoid.

As educated adults with years of job experience, we possess a very large data bank in our heads about what is right, what is wrong, what works, and what does not. This helps us make good judgments, helps keep us safe, and helps ensure our very survival—a critical ability that's invaluable most of the time but that can impede and even derail divergent thinking.

CAUTION

## DON'T DOUSE THE SPARK

Scott Adams, in his famous Dilbert comic strip, immortalized the practice of judging ideas too quickly. A young engineer who had worked in his job only one day went to his boss with a new idea. The boss is next pictured with a fire hose dousing him with water. In the last frame Dilbert says, "The first idea is always the toughest," and Wally says, "The urge eventually goes away." The new engineer will likely have more ideas, but it's unlikely he will share them with the boss. His ideas can never be used to help the company.

All employees (but especially, the experts) need to understand the distinction between divergent thinking and convergent thinking and they need to learn to suspend at certain times their tendency to converge, in order to allow new ideas to flourish. Children are naturally divergent in their thinking because they don't yet have much knowledge and experience against which to judge new ideas. We must learn to become more "childlike" by asking, as children do, "What's right about this idea?" and staying away from those harmful killer phrases.

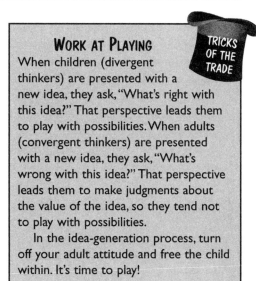

**WORK AT PLAYING**

*TRICKS OF THE TRADE*

When children (divergent thinkers) are presented with a new idea, they ask, "What's right with this idea?" That perspective leads them to play with possibilities. When adults (convergent thinkers) are presented with a new idea, they ask, "What's wrong with this idea?" That perspective leads them to make judgments about the value of the idea, so they tend not to play with possibilities.

In the idea-generation process, turn off your adult attitude and free the child within. It's time to play!

In short, we must learn not to say no and instead to say yes.

Fortunately, saying yes to new ideas can have even more than just the opposite effect of saying no. It can be empowering, not only for the person generating the idea, but also for the organization as a whole.

Dr. Richard Stieglitz, former president of RGS Associates, Inc. in Arlington, Virginia knows the great multiplying power of just saying yes. In his book, *Taming the Dragons of Change* (Publish America, 2006), he gives the following story illustrating the power of just saying yes.

> In the early 1990s, several years before websites became commonplace, a young engineer who had been with us only six months walked into my office and asked: 'Can I build a public website for the company?' Since we never had installed a firewall and website, I asked the usual management questions: 'What will it cost, and how long will it take?' Having evaluated the requirements thoroughly, he responded instantly: 'About $75,000 for the server and software, and a week for me to install them.' After hesitating a moment, he added: 'Oh, by the way, we'll need a T1 line too, which will cost about $4,000 a month.' I cringed at the thought of a $75,000 investment plus recurring expenses of $4,000 a month. Reluctantly, I said YES and

approved the investment. The actual costs were over $90,000 with phone line installation and other unexpected extras. After the server and software arrived six weeks later, the employee struggled for weeks to make the site work. Others pitched in to help too. The team tried everything they knew. They came to work early, stayed late, and worked weekends. Every painful step forward was followed by a setback, until it finally worked! The benefits to the company of that small 'YES' were enormous, giving us an edge in the application of web technologies that continues today."

In his second book, *Taming the Dragons of Change in Business* (Acuity Publishing, 2009), Stieglitz says, "YES is a collaboration message. When you say YES, you strengthen relationships. YES empowers people to achieve more while NO is a message of rejection. NO forces your teammates to defend their ideas, or to find another way. Their loyalty to you will determine how many NOs they'll accept before seeking employment elsewhere. Based on the number of people who move from one company to another in the relationship economy, there are too many NOs and not enough YESes."

> **SMART**
>
> **PROMOTE A POSITIVE PERSPECTIVE**
>
> **MANAGING**
>
> Saying yes nurtures innovation and drives results beyond individual contributions. I say, yes to you, you add a yes to someone else, and others observe and build on our yesses until results exceed expectations.

A great illustration of the killer phrase, "We've tried that before," comes from the mathematician August Möbius (inventor of the Möbius strip). Over 150 years ago he put a hungry pike fish in a very large aquarium, placed a bottomless five-gallon glass jar in the same aquarium with the pike on the outside, and put minnows inside the jar. Then he watched what happened. The pike tried over and over again to eat the minnows, but all it got for its efforts was a sore nose. Eventually the pike gave up and settled to the bottom of the aquarium and stopped trying. The fish must have reasoned, "I've tried that and it didn't work." Then Möbius lifted the bottomless jar out of the aquarium, allowing the minnows to swim freely throughout the aquarium. The pike never tried to get the minnows—and eventually died of starvation! The fish did not realize that the conditions had changed drastically and it was now possible to eat the minnows.

If someone says to you, "We've tried that before," I recommend you accept his or her experience as a fact. However, you might reply, "I'm sure that was true at the time, but let's examine what might've changed since then. Technology changes, customer needs change, regulations change, and what didn't make any sense at all at that time might make perfect sense today."

Killer phrases can be devastating for creativity and innovation. If individuals decide not to share their ideas, those ideas are useless. And teams and groups cannot generate ideas; only individuals can do that! Innovation is a social process requiring individuals to participate by sharing their ideas. If the climate for innovation is poisoned, people may choose not to share their ideas.

---

## USING AN ANALOGY TO DISCOURAGE NEGATIVE REACTIONS

In my workshops I ask someone who has at least two children to think about when his or her first child was born. "Remember how beautiful your baby was and how proud you were!" And then I ask if anyone to whom the new parent showed the baby ever said that it was ugly. Of course everyone laughs, and the person always says, "No that never happened." Then I ask, "If that had happened, would you have shown your second baby to the same person?" And the answer is always "No, I would never do that."

The point is that your ideas are like your infants because you gave birth to them. If they get judged negatively, especially in a public setting like a group meeting, you will never reveal any subsequent ideas to the same group.

---

Ideas that are not expressed can never be used to help the company. Let me strongly recommend that you commit to saying at least three good things about every new idea that is put forward before you say anything negative. If you are in a leadership position, you might want to lead by modeling the behavior you want others to adopt and then gently enforcing it in your group meetings. This is such a simple thing to do that it is amazing how many people never give this a try.

In all of my years running research groups, I always found that the first people to judge an idea negatively were always the technical experts

---

### TARGET SNAP JUDGMENTS

This technique mentioned earlier works well if set up properly. Have every member of the group crumple a sheet of paper into a ball. Then ask them to throw their crumpled creations at anyone who judges an idea prematurely in your meeting.

Here is a list of rules for paper balls that you might want to put on display for your group:

Rule 1. No hard things inside!

Rule 2. Don't dip them in the coffee or water!

Rule 3. Don't set them on fire!

Rule 4. If you get pelted, keep the projectiles—you may need them later.

Rule 5. If you are the target, it just means you are an expert, because usually only experts make judgments in public.

---

who knew so very much and who had so much experience. Ironically, it's just those people who you wish would use that experience and knowledge to figure out how to make ideas work, rather than to explain how ideas could not work! For some strange reason, people may delight in demolishing ideas put forth by their peers, usually in public, because it makes them appear so knowledgeable and smart. This reaction puts a big damper on idea generation!

## Pitfall #3: Stopping with the First Good Idea

The first good idea is never the best. If it was that easy to come up with the idea, there's little doubt that your competitors have already thought of it too. Also, the first idea is generally derived from brainstorming. Effective as it is, brainstorming isn't set up to break through our thinking patterns. Most often during a brainstorming session, the "usual" ideas emerge. Perhaps they are slightly modified, but they are almost never the truly unexpected ideas that are needed to surpass the competition. We like to illustrate this concept by presenting a problem to participants and asking for their ideas to solve it. (We develop this strategy in Chapter 8.)

We begin with brainstorming. Typically participants begin by proposing conventional suggestions. We then introduce a pattern-breaking tool (described in Chapter 8) and have them apply this new tool to the problem. Instantly they are able to think of highly innovative ideas. The results show that the most innovative ideas come after the participants have run out of ideas by just brainstorming. When they break their thinking patterns, they generate more innovative ideas.

The first ideas to solve any problem always come from within the walls of our "thinking box." Only by going outside those walls can we readily discover the innovative ideas just waiting to be found by our competitors. We must be the first to find these ideas and then implement them if we wish to stay ahead in the marketplace.

There's always a great temptation to move ahead quickly when under pressure to solve a problem or create a new product or service, because of the pressures of the business. This can be a big mistake, because it can lead you to stop with the first good idea.

If we should stop simply at brainstorming, we can get new and useful ideas, yes, but they will not likely be innovative or unexpected. Thinking outside

> **Box** The limits of conventional thinking. The walls of our "mental box" are composed of our logic and **KEY TERM** assumptions about the problem being solved, constraints reinforced by our patterned thinking. The term seems to have developed from the nine-dots puzzle, which consists of connecting nine dots arranged in a three-by-three shape by drawing only four connected straight lines. This is possible only if you draw outside of the confines of the square area formed by the dots—a box constructed by our minds.

the box gives us the unexpected ideas that keep us ahead of the competition, whereas staying within the box simply produces ideas that any of our competitors probably already have or, if not, can produce as quickly as we can. Staying ahead of the competition means going the extra step and generating and implementing unexpected ideas before the others.

## DUMP BEFORE YOU JUMP

Brainstorming as usually practiced just empties our mental box of all the usual ideas. It is not engineered to break our patterns of thought and get us out of our thinking boxes.

A fact I learned through hard experience is that we cannot get "out of the box" unless we empty the box first. Brainstorming to empty the box is critically important and must be completed first. All of the obvious ideas need to be captured and honored so we don't keep repeating them as we begin to think outside the box.

At the DuPont Center for Creativity and Innovation, we created a comic book titled *Are We Creative Yet?* This book contains stories from employees about different aspects of innovation, illustrated by cartoons provided by the late Bob Thaves, cartoonist for the Frank and Ernest comic strip.

One of the comics has to do with stopping with the first good idea. It pictures a herd of lemmings jumping off a cliff into the sea. One of the lemmings turns to the other and says, "I don't know, there must be a sale or something!" The lemmings were blindly following after the first idea. This pitfall is particularly damaging if the first good idea came from the boss and the subordinates don't feel they can question or challenge the idea.

I once opened a Chinese fortune cookie, and the strip of paper inside read, "The best ideas come after you have run out of ideas." Ancient Chinese wisdom that makes more and more sense now!

## Pitfall #4: Obeying Rules That Don't Exist

Many times we disable ourselves by assuming we cannot do something, when in fact there is no reason to believe that. We may assume that we must obey some rule when actually there is no such rule at all. Every organization has been saddled with this deterrent to innovative thinking.

For example, a global chemical company was in the business of making carpet yarn that went into some of the finest carpets in the world. It made every single component used in the carpet. One of its unwritten rules was "We will never compete with our customers," which of course meant the company would never produce and sell carpets. The managers remained content to supply the components and let their customers make and sell the carpets. However, as times got tough, their customers were not bound by the same thinking, and they decided to backward integrate. Using off-the-shelf fiber-spinning equipment, they began producing their own carpet fiber—and now the chemical company is no longer in the business of making carpet yarn.

Another example comes from the U.S. Army Corps of Engineers, the Vicksburg, Mississippi. District. In 1974 the U.S. Army examined its battlefield practices to see which practices might have outlived their usefulness. They found that when the cannon were fired on the battlefield, a soldier was standing behind the cannon with both arms in the air. His

## "WE DON'T DO THAT"

A classic story in psychology classes tells of an interesting experiment. A psychologist put four monkeys into a cage, with a pole in the center with bananas on top. As the monkeys scampered up the pole and got close to the bananas, he squirted them with cold water from a hose. They didn't like that, so they learned to stop trying to get the bananas. The psychologist then put away the water hose, never to use it again, and began changing the monkeys out. He replaced an experienced monkey with a new monkey, who, upon seeing the bananas, began to scamper up the pole. The experienced monkeys in the cage slapped him down and wouldn't let him go up the pole. One by one all of the experienced monkeys were replaced. Although none of the new monkeys had been sprayed, they would not climb the pole. Each had learned that "we don't do that." This experiment illustrates the power of learning to obey rules derived from conditions that no longer exist.

purpose was to hold the horses that had been used to move the cannon around the battlefield. Horses hadn't been used in 40 years, but a soldier was standing in position to hold their reins!

People in an organization learn what behavior is acceptable and what is not through stories and experiences. These lessons can hinder innovation if they keep people from considering new things because in the past the same or similar things did not work out well. It's a good idea every five years or so to take a look at ideas that were shelved earlier to see if the time might be right for them.

## DON'T RESTRICT YOUR THINKING WITH ASSUMPTIONS

There's a Gary Larson comic that shows two cowboys crouched behind covered wagons as flaming arrows head their way. One says to the other, "Hey, they're lighting their arrows! Can they do that?" Hiding behind canvas and wood makes sense to the cowboys if they assume that Indians will be simply shooting pointed sticks. But when the Indians, not restricting their thinking, start fighting with fire, taking cover behind flammable materials suddenly becomes dangerous.

Some cultures send strong messages that everything must be explicitly permitted or else it cannot be done. This alone is a surefire killer of innovation. How ridiculous! Like these comic cowboys, people in these cultures can be victims of the restrictions they assume and caught by surprise when their competitors, like these Indians, do not accept such restrictions when they innovate for a competitive edge.

### Pitfall #5: Failing to Get Sponsorship and Build Coalitions

Failure to get sponsorship and build coalitions is one of the "silent killers" of innovation. Of course, the reason is that without organizational support nothing of importance can happen with good ideas. There is always a constituency or a person lying in wait to torpedo the idea.

The strategy for avoiding this pitfall is what I sometimes call getting the "bandit on the train" so that he won't dynamite the track. Imagine that you are a passenger on a train in the American West in 1891 and your biggest fear is that bandits on horseback are going to dynamite the track and derail the train. How do you prevent that? How about buying the bandits tickets and making them passengers! Instantly the bandits become vested in helping make the trip successful and generally will not stand in the way of progress.

So, how do you go about getting the bandit on the train? The first step is to identify the bandit or bandits. The bandits are almost always those people or constituencies whose support you must have in order for your idea to progress. Typically this means the boss or at least the person who has the power to allocate dollars and people to a particular project. It might even mean a member of a vocal minority whose support you need.

---

**SMART**

**MANAGING**

### GET THE BANDIT ON THE TRAIN

When we began the Center for Creativity and Innovation at DuPont, we were asked to facilitate a three-day workshop with 31 participants dealing with an important commercial problem. The director of this business unit kicked off our workshop with a wonderful presentation and dinner at the five-star Hotel DuPont. Then he left for a business meeting. He returned after three days to learn what had happened. Unfortunately, he disagreed with everything we had decided to do, and nothing was ever accomplished as a result of that meeting.

I decided we would never again be involved in a workshop in which "the bandit wasn't on the train." That workshop was a waste of time and energy, and the experience greatly frustrated the participants.

---

## Skills Needed by New Product Team Leaders

Carol Kobza, former Knowledge and Idea Manager at Hallmark Cards Inc., led a very successful innovation team in 2004 to help enrich its

## GET THE POWER YOU NEED

Detroit Edison, an electric utility, had a big problem—selecting sites for electrical substations for future growth. The real estate division would study the demographics and predict how the population was likely to expand. Then the company would buy up small tracts of land in the direction of expected growth. When the population grew as anticipated and the need arose, the utility would construct a substation. When members of the community realized what was happening, they would file lawsuits to stop the construction, costing the company lots of money and causing delays in construction.

During the planning for a workshop, a Detroit Edison executive noted that a particular person was the leader in bringing about the lawsuits. He decided that she was a key "bandit" that the company needed to bring onto the train for this workshop. She was invited, participated completely, and helped craft solutions that met everyone's needs without lawsuits. At the end of this workshop, she commented, "This is the first time I've ever been asked for my opinion, and it is great to have been able to contribute to a good solution."

Never underestimate the power of identifying the "bandits" and making sure they're on the train as you begin your problem-solving journey.

product line with totally new offerings. Below is her list of the key skills that new product development team leaders need to possess.

1. **Objective decision making.** Evaluate ideas based on clear, agreed-upon criteria.

2. **Communication on the run.** Listen to the team members and keep them informed all day every day. Describe ideas with enthusiasm.

3. **Leadership.** Help others feel optimistic and confident that the project will be successful. Make all individuals feel that they and their opinions matter.

4. **Concept development.** Develop the art of writing concept statements. Be open to ideas, and know when you see one.

5. **Innovation skills beyond creativity.** Use influence and the ability to gather the right people for the team. Sleuth out the expertise required inside and outside the organization. Learn and apply knowledge and understanding of innovation as a discipline.

Members of innovation teams need these key attributes, beyond the obvious:

- Optimism
- Open-mindedness
- Unwillingness to give up
- Desire to improve the company rather than complain about it
- Willingness to question assumptions

---

**SMART**

**MANAGING**

### MAKE DECISIONS IN ADVANCE

One outstanding lesson for Carol Kobza and her team was that decisions must be based on clear criteria agreed to upfront. All too often in organizations, decisions and choices are made against a set of criteria that are usually not discussed before the decision or choice is made. This most often leads to squabbles over the decision or choice itself, squabbles that could have been avoided had the criteria been agreed to before making the decision. What Kobza so elegantly points out is that those criteria must be clear, understood, agreed to, and most of all public among those who have a vote. Then individuals with their personal biases and hidden agendas will not be making the decisions; it will be the open and public criteria that make them.

This point is so important to Kobza that she cited one decision as an example. The team created an idea that all the members naturally loved. They normally would have decided to move ahead with scale-up since it was their idea. However, when they evaluated the idea against their criteria, they decided to kill the project since it did not meet the criteria.

---

## Manager's Checklist for Chapter 2

☑ Teach your team the importance of divergent thinking and convergent thinking—and the need to keep the two separate.

☑ Be sure the right problem is defined before brainstorming possible solutions.

☑ Stop judging ideas too quickly; force yourself to say at least three good things about every new idea before you say anything negative. Insist on this behavior in your team meetings as well.

☑ Refuse to accept the first good idea as the best idea. Dig for more.

☑ Examine your business practices and processes to see what isn't appropriate anymore. Don't be the one caught "holding the horses."

☑ Carefully search to find all the "bandits" for your projects and find ways to enlist their support early. People will help your project succeed if you "put them on the train."

☑ When selections must be made, be sure the criteria to be used to make the selection are clear, agreed to by the stakeholders, and public.

Chapter 3

# Creative Thinking

**W**hen I ask workshop participants to raise their hands if they feel they are creative, only about 20 percent raise their hands! Then I ask how many dream at night—and, of course, most everyone raises their hand. Who creates the fantastic plots, who creates those ridiculous characters, and where do all of those totally unexpected things come from? The answer, of course, is your own brain, because you are creative! Our challenge is to have creative ideas while we are awake, not just while we are asleep.

## Cultivating Natural Creativity

What are you doing during the day when you have your best ideas?

Chic Thompson, in *What a Great Idea! 2.0* (Sterling Publishing Co., 2007), lists the top 10 "idea-friendly times" based on informal surveys of his clients. Here is his list. Please note that "while at work" is not on the list—at least not in so many words.

10. While performing manual labor
 9. While listening to a sermon
 8. On waking up in the middle of the night
 7. While exercising
 6. During leisure reading
 5. During a boring meeting

4. While falling asleep or waking up

3. While sitting on the toilet

2. While commuting to work

1. While showering or taking a bath

What do all of these activities have in common? Your brain is in neutral and you don't have to think deeply about what you're doing. That's probably why "at work" is not on the list. Your brain is not in neutral or relaxed.

These results also support the notion that we need idea time in our environment for innovation. Idea time (time for idea generation) is one of the dimensions of the climate for innovation that will be described more completely in Chapter 10.

One of the landmark books on creative thinking was *The Art of Thought,* written in 1926 by Graham Wallas. In his book he outlined four phases of the creative process, as follows:

- Preparation—learning the background and being totally absorbed by the problem
- Incubation—taking a break
- Illumination—getting the "Ah Ha!"
- Verification—testing the idea

Think about how you've solved problems. You undoubtedly progressed through each of these phases, probably without even realizing it.

What is creativity? Creativity is normally thought of as the ability to create novelty. However, in the real world it must be more than that. I believe it must be the ability to

> **GET IT IN WRITING**
> Capture your dreams to benefit from that source of creativity. Keep a sticky-note pad on your nightstand to capture ideas as you wake up during the night and in the morning. Your subconscious mind never sleeps; it accepts instructions from your conscious mind, and it will work on any problem you give it as you are falling asleep.
>
> **TOOLS**

develop new, useful, and *unexpected* alternatives to solve problems or take advantage of opportunities. Please note that I have emphasized the word "unexpected" because it is doing the unexpected that will truly keep you

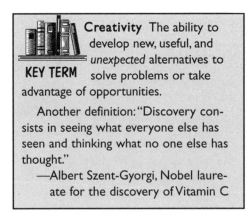

**IDEA SPRINGS FROM SLEEP**

**FOR EXAMPLE**

The DuPont Center for Creativity and Innovation produced videotapes showcasing innovation successes in the company. One success was the story of Floyd Ragsdale, a machine operator in the Kevlar plant.

There was a problem with a vacuum hose carrying away dilute acid from part of the manufacturing process. The hose was collapsing on the inside due to the vacuum, which stopped the process from running, but it looked perfectly fine from the outside. A number of engineers and the hose provider had been trying to solve this problem, without much success.

As Ragsdale tells it, "When I went to sleep that night the problem was throbbing in my head like a toothache, it just wouldn't go away. I dreamed of a Slinky®, you know the spring toy that would walk downstairs. My children happen to have one, so I took it to work and put it on the inside of the vacuum hose and it fixed the problem!"

Floyd certainly knew all about the problem and was totally absorbed by it even as he fell asleep (Preparation). The Incubation period occurred while he was asleep, as did the Illumination or "Ah Ha!" moment. Verification came when he tested his idea the next morning and solved the problem.

ahead of your competition. You may have seen something one of your competitors has produced, and you might well have said, "Why didn't we think of that?" It's clear that the competitor was able to do the unexpected before you were. One of my most important learnings was that unexpected alternatives cannot be developed by thinking the same old way; all we get is the same old ideas. In Chapter 8 you will learn a number of ways to get unexpected ideas by breaking your thinking patterns—that is, thinking outside the box.

**KEY TERM** **Creativity** The ability to develop new, useful, and *unexpected* alternatives to solve problems or take advantage of opportunities.

Another definition: "Discovery consists in seeing what everyone else has seen and thinking what no one else has thought."
—Albert Szent-Gyorgi, Nobel laureate for the discovery of Vitamin C

# Ideas from Brainstorming

Brainstorming is a group creativity technique designed to generate a large number of ideas to solve a problem. Alex Osborn began brainstorming internally as a founder of BBDO, the New York City advertising firm in the late 1930s, and popularized it in his book, *Applied Imagination,* in 1953. This landmark book was republished in 1957, 1963, and 1967 and has been translated into 14 languages. His four rules for brainstorming have remained consistent:

1. Go for quantity of ideas. The more ideas, the more likely one that will work.
2. Withhold judgment. Premature judgment stops the flow of ideas.
3. Build on the ideas of others. Ideas from one person will spark new ideas from others.
4. Seek wild ideas. Invite one or two "wild cards" to your sessions. These are people known to think differently and usually not experts in the area of the problem, so they don't know that some things are "impossible."

> **Brainstorming** A group creativity technique designed to generate ideas, in which group members **KEY TERM** freely and spontaneously present ideas, in a positive environment in which critical or negative thinking is suspended.

## Why Typical Brainstorming Doesn't Work Well

You undoubtedly have participated in so-called brainstorming meetings that resulted in nothing important. You may have even been guilty of leading such meetings yourself.

Brainstorming has earned a bad name primarily because of the totally ineffective traditional process that has been taught and used for years. The facilitator stands at a flip chart with a marker in hand and announces that he or she will write down any idea that anyone contributes. Someone, usually an extrovert, finally has the courage to offer up an idea, which the facilitator writes on the pad, usually changing the words to meet his or her own biases. Then, another person usually explains, in great detail, what's wrong with the idea. Most or all of the others are reluctant to say anything for fear that their ideas also will be judged negatively in public. When other ideas are offered, many times they're in the same vein as the first idea.

What's wrong with this process? Answer—most everything!

1. In a group the introverts are reluctant to speak, so only the extroverts contribute. That means that 50 percent of the creativity is lost from the start.
2. All ideas must flow through the facilitator's pen, which slows things down. The processing is serial processing, with very few ideas being captured.
3. The public nature of idea capture invites immediate judgment because everyone can see the ideas and can comment, usually negatively.
4. What happens is groupthink, because the prevailing line of thought is in everyone's head and new ideas generally fall into that same area.

---

### EMPTY THE BOX BY BRAINSTORMING TO EXHAUSTION

**TOOLS**

We have found that brainstorming with sticky notes will result in about 20 ideas per participant when the session is facilitated by an expert. We learned early that one cannot get out of the "box" until the box is first emptied, and we believe that "brainstorming to exhaustion" using sticky notes is the most effective way to quickly achieve this. If brainstorming is not taken to exhaustion, then a number of easy and obvious ideas will remain to be pulled from the box, and they will cause pattern-breaking thinking to be less effective.

---

## Use Sticky Notes for Effective Brainstorming

Post-it® notes are a wonderful 3M invention that allows groups to implement fully the four rules of brainstorming first proposed by Osborn. Here's how this version of brainstorming works.

Every participant has his or her pad of sticky notes and a pen. The facilitator makes sure all members of the group understand the problem and asks them to write down a minimum of 10 specific and actionable ideas to solve the problem, one idea per note page. They are to do this without any discussion.

Next, the participants share their ideas in groups of two or three, and each small group is challenged to create five new ideas by building on each other's ideas. This process of using sticky notes is vastly superior to the old method of facilitator and flip chart because it avoids the four pitfalls of the traditional method. Using this version of brainstorming:

1. Introverts contribute equally as much as extroverts because all participants express their ideas in silence.

2. All participants write at the same time—the processing is parallel—so there is a huge increase in the quantity of ideas.

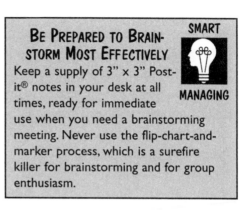

**BE PREPARED TO BRAINSTORM MOST EFFECTIVELY**
Keep a supply of 3" x 3" Post-it® notes in your desk at all times, ready for immediate use when you need a brainstorming meeting. Never use the flip-chart-and-marker process, which is a surefire killer for brainstorming and for group enthusiasm.

3. The private nature of writing ideas prevents immediate negative judgment by others.

4. Groupthink is avoided because each participant is thinking in his or her individual channels of thought without being influenced by the others.

## The Ladder of Abstraction and Idea Generation

The ladder of abstraction (Figure 3-1) will help your team create more specific and therefore more actionable and useful ideas than normally produced in a brainstorming session. The ladder of abstraction was given to us by Alfred Korzybski, a Polish immigrant who is widely cred-

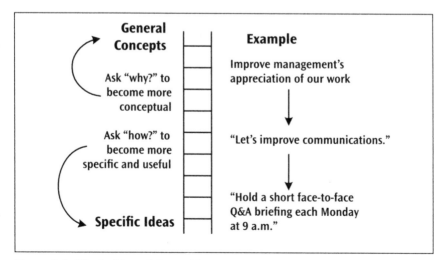

Figure 3-1. The ladder of abstraction

ited with creating the science of semantics. He said, "The more concrete and specific your ideas are, the more powerful and useful they are."

Figure 3-1 shows abstract concepts at the top of the ladder and specific and actionable ideas at the bottom of the ladder. Whenever any idea is put forth, it can be placed at some level on this imaginary ladder. To drive down the ladder, we simply ask "how?" questions of the idea.

For example, if our problem is to improve the perceived status of our department within the organization, someone might suggest the idea to improve management's appreciation for the work we do. That suggestion is more conceptual than specific and belongs near the top of the ladder. To make it more useful, we need to make it more specific and actionable by answering the "how?" question. Asking "how?" might lead to a specific idea, such as "Let's improve communications." This idea is more specific than the original one, but still rather general. If we ask the "how?" question again, someone might then say, "Hold a short face-to-face Q&A meeting every Monday at 9 a.m." You can readily see that this idea is more specific, more actionable, and more useful than the preceding two.

An easy test for specific and actionable is to ask yourself, "Is the idea specific enough that I would know how to get started if it were my only job on Monday morning?"

---

**PUSH IDEAS DOWN THE LADDER**

One of the reasons why brainstorming meetings are sometimes ineffective is that many of the ideas put forward are really just concepts near the top of the ladder and are not specific enough to convey how to get started. You can avoid this problem and make your next brainstorming meeting more effective by displaying the ladder of abstraction, Figure 3-1, and explaining how it can be useful.

You might draw the ladder on a flip chart and place each idea on sticky notes at the level of abstraction that the group considers appropriate. You might then insist that every idea become more specific and actionable by asking "how?" questions, relocating the sticky notes toward the bottom of the ladder. This will help guarantee that your meeting will result in more actionable output.

# Ideas from Pattern-Breaking Thinking

We call the out-of-the-box thinking that is needed to create unexpected ideas "pattern-breaking" thinking because our thinking patterns (habits—or ways of thinking) keep us within the walls of our mental boxes. We must break these mental walls to get out of the box.

Our thinking patterns are usually beneficial, because they enable us to live more efficiently. For example, you didn't have to take time to think about how to put on your clothes this morning. You could have put your socks on after you put on your shoes, but you didn't have to think about it, because habits increase our efficiency at everything we do.

However, our same patterned thinking also works to keep us in our mental "box." One of the walls of our thinking box is made up of our assumptions, the things we assume about the problem at hand. One of the effective techniques is to identify our hidden assumptions and deny them, thereby mentally punching through the walls of our box to get outside. (We will discuss this technique in Chapter 4.)

# Ideas from Suggestion Systems

Alan G. Robinson and Sam Stern (*Corporate Creativity*, Berrett-Koehler Publishers, 1997) note that the first recorded suggestion system to promote creativity in companies was instituted in 1880 by William Denny at his shipbuilding firm in Scotland. He set up a two-person awards committee to decide which suggestions were worthy of the money the company would pay for each accepted idea. By 1887 more than 600 ideas had been received, 196 of which were judged worthy of acceptance.

Denny's system quickly generated interest and was widely copied throughout Great Britain and Europe. As it turns out, this system, effective since it was the first, came with two major limitations. First, the ideas submitted had no "home," since no problem or need had been stated to serve as a target. Second, the system depended on external rewards to stimulate creativity. We now know from our own experience as well as those of worldwide experts that motivation based on the promise of a reward will stimulate activity, but it is the wrong way to stimulate creativity. You will get what you pay for (lots of ideas), but it will not be what you want (high-quality ideas with bottom-line business merit).

In her book *Growing up Creative* (Crown Publishers, 1989), Teresa Amabile describes experiments she ran with children showing how competition for a reward destroys creativity. She invited girls between the ages of 7 and 11 in her apartment complex to attend an art party, half on Saturday and the other half on Sunday. At the Saturday party she showed the girls three prizes that would be raffled off at the end of the party, and then she asked each child to make a collage. She did the same at the Sunday party, except that before the collage making she told the girls that prizes would be awarded to the three who made the best collages. Later she had artists rate all the collages for creativity. The collages from the noncompetitive Saturday group were judged to be more creative than those from the competitive Sunday group.

Why? When people create anything hoping for acceptance, they usually create things that they believe will be acceptable to established authority, which means they are usually more mainstream and therefore less creative and less innovative.

I'm reminded of the simple yet insightfully elegant quote from Dr. W. Edeards Deming (and others): "Every system is perfectly designed to give you the results you get." People will game the system: that's why you will get what you pay for, but not necessarily what you want.

Robinson and Stern recount that in 1892 John Patterson started the NCR Corp. based on the invention of the cash register. Patterson had the idea that if he were to consider the employees at the top of the inverted organizational pyramid with himself at the tip on the bottom, then he had a "hundred-headed brain" that he could use to improve the company. He created an elaborate system of monetary awards and celebrations for ideas that saved the company money. By 1904 the number of suggestions had risen to an

**SMART MANAGING**

**IF YOU PAY FOR IDEAS, EXPECT QUANTITY, NOT QUALITY**

For managers the lesson is clear; to ensure *less* creative ideas, set up a competition and promise a prize to the winner. For example, a major privately held U.S. company instituted an idea management system in which they paid employees for ideas up front. It was soon discovered that several employees were submitting large quantities of very poor quality ideas simply to fatten their paychecks.

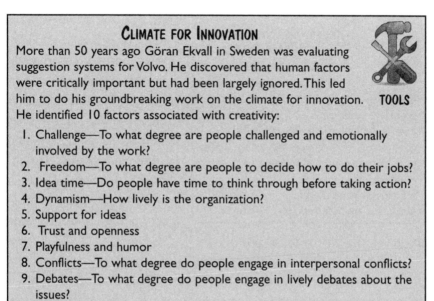

## CLIMATE FOR INNOVATION

More than 50 years ago Göran Ekvall in Sweden was evaluating suggestion systems for Volvo. He discovered that human factors were critically important but had been largely ignored. This led him to do his groundbreaking work on the climate for innovation. **TOOLS** He identified 10 factors associated with creativity:

1. Challenge—To what degree are people challenged and emotionally involved by the work?
2. Freedom—To what degree are people to decide how to do their jobs?
3. Idea time—Do people have time to think through before taking action?
4. Dynamism—How lively is the organization?
5. Support for ideas
6. Trust and openness
7. Playfulness and humor
8. Conflicts—To what degree do people engage in interpersonal conflicts?
9. Debates—To what degree do people engage in lively debates about the issues?
10. Risk taking—Is it OK to fail?

His work has resulted in our current validated assessment of climate, the Situational Outlook Questionnaire (see Chapter 11).

average of about two per employee. However, upon Patterson's death in 1922, performance of the suggestion system began a steady decline and it eventually fell into disuse. This pattern of initial interest followed by eventual disuse was repeated throughout the country. Through the years most companies have tried the traditional suggestion box, usually attached to a wall in the office or the plant and usually gathering chewing

## SURPRISE COST OF SAFETY

The safety supervisor of a paper plant decided to promote safety by offering an incentive to plant employees: he would raffle off a pickup truck if the plant met its annual safety goal. He gave every employee a free ticket for the raffle.

Did the employees meet the safety goal? Of course! When there's significant money or value in achieving a measurable goal, people will find a way to do it. However, as the plant neared the goal, employees stopped working—because they were afraid of having an accident. Productivity fell dramatically, but the safety goal was met and someone won the truck! Please recall that important truth: "Every system is perfectly designed to give you the results you get."

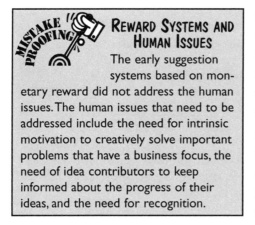

**REWARD SYSTEMS AND HUMAN ISSUES**
The early suggestion systems based on monetary reward did not address the human issues. The human issues that need to be addressed include the need for intrinsic motivation to creatively solve important problems that have a business focus, the need of idea contributors to keep informed about the progress of their ideas, and the need for recognition.

gum wrappers. Whenever I see a suggestion box in a client's organization, I know immediately that the system doesn't work. When I ask my Executive MBA class participants how many have suggestion systems in their companies, usually about 50 percent raise their hands. Then I ask how many of those actually produce good results, and all the hands go down.

Suggestion systems require special attention to the human aspects in order for them to produce the desired results. What's needed, of course, is an improved communication system between workers and management so that the workers have a chance to suggest what might make the company more innovative, a better place to work, more productive, or more profitable. What's missing in most systems is that upper managers do not understand the human side of suggestion systems, which is what makes for success or failure.

Here are three points to keep in mind:

- Employees want to know that their suggestions are aimed at a worthwhile problem to be solved.
- Employees don't want their suggestions to disappear; at a minimum they want to be recognized and thanked for their suggestions.
- Managers don't want to waste their time reading what they consider to be stupid suggestions that aren't aimed at a business issue and don't make any sense.

The mistake that many organizations make is to initiate a suggestion system with great fanfare and attention, urging all employees to contribute suggestions. There might even be a contest for the most ideas from each area. Usually a panel of managers (or sadly, just one person) is appointed to evaluate the ideas, which initially pour in like an avalanche, because these have been pent up from years when there was no welcome outlet.

### FIND OUT WHAT WORKS FROM EMPLOYEES

SMART

MANAGING

"One has to assume, first, that the individual human being at work knows better than anyone else what makes him or her more productive . . . even in routine work the only true expert is the person who does the job."
—Peter Drucker

On an annual employee satisfaction survey run in the mid-1980s at a DuPont fibers plant, one of the hourly workers said the following, "For 20 years you have paid for my hands and you could have had my head for free but you never asked." Clearly there was no mechanism for communicating ideas to management, at least that this employee recognized and was willing to use.

Make sure the channels of communication are open with a system that works. You don't have to invest in a software solution (although data shows they produce an enormous ROI); just implement some of the straightforward principles to be described below.

The task of evaluating ideas becomes very burdensome to already overworked managers, which causes either a quick rejection or a long delay in any response. More "no" responses than "yesses" and, worse still, no response at all and the idea flow slows and then stops. Ideas are replaced by cynicism and the system is usually abandoned after a year or two.

This scenario is as predictable as death and taxes. You will want to avoid setting up a system destined for failure like this.

One such notable failure was experienced by a travel reservations system located in Atlanta. The company took every single step outlined above, especially the quick "no" response to practically every idea submitted. Predictably, idea submissions slowed to a trickle, then stopped altogether, and the program was abandoned within six months. That company has since been merged with a competitor.

## A Suggestion System That Actually Works

There are a number of software packages to help you implement an effective suggestion system. Idea Central (*www.imaginatik.com*) is a very comprehensive system for large organizations. It has a track record of success with very large ROI demonstrated. The company has effectively dealt with the human issues that cause poorly thought-out suggestion systems to fail, and the software greatly simplifies and reduces the bookkeeping required to administer the system. Idea-Tool-Kit (*www.biztrain.com*) offers an inexpensive software solution. A structured "Bright Ideas Campaign" methodology without software is even less expensive (*www.chartcourse.com*).

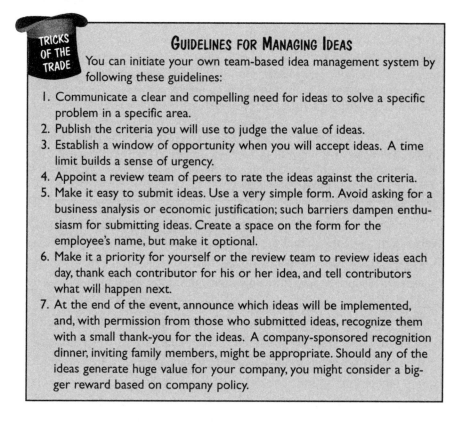

**TRICKS OF THE TRADE**

## GUIDELINES FOR MANAGING IDEAS

You can initiate your own team-based idea management system by following these guidelines:

1. Communicate a clear and compelling need for ideas to solve a specific problem in a specific area.
2. Publish the criteria you will use to judge the value of ideas.
3. Establish a window of opportunity when you will accept ideas. A time limit builds a sense of urgency.
4. Appoint a review team of peers to rate the ideas against the criteria.
5. Make it easy to submit ideas. Use a very simple form. Avoid asking for a business analysis or economic justification; such barriers dampen enthusiasm for submitting ideas. Create a space on the form for the employee's name, but make it optional.
6. Make it a priority for yourself or the review team to review ideas each day, thank each contributor for his or her idea, and tell contributors what will happen next.
7. At the end of the event, announce which ideas will be implemented, and, with permission from those who submitted ideas, recognize them with a small thank-you for the ideas. A company-sponsored recognition dinner, inviting family members, might be appropriate. Should any of the ideas generate huge value for your company, you might consider a bigger reward based on company policy.

# TRIZ—Left-Brained Idea Generation

In the interest of rounding out this chapter on creativity, I am including the following short section describing TRIZ, one of the newest methods of idea generation.

What if you could get all the greatest inventors in the world into your brainstorming session? Thanks to the pioneering work of Genrich Altshuller, an ingenious patent examiner in the former Soviet Union, you can now do this with TRIZ, which is the Russian acronym for "Theory of Inventive Problem Solving."

In reviewing patents, Altshuller realized that the breakthrough patents were those that solved a fundamental contradiction, for example "soft but durable" and "lightweight but strong." Altshuller started his work in 1947, but the results were suppressed and only became known to

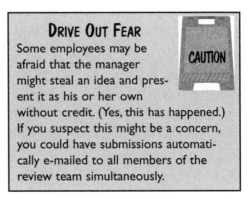

**DRIVE OUT FEAR**

Some employees may be afraid that the manager might steal an idea and present it as his or her own without credit. (Yes, this has happened.) If you suspect this might be a concern, you could have submissions automatically e-mailed to all members of the review team simultaneously.

the Western world in 1990 after *perestroika*. TRIZ is now practiced by many major corporations.

## How It Works

In studying breakthrough patents, Altshuller identified 40 inventive principles. These principles were developed by analyzing how inventors resolved fundamental contradictions. In 50 years of continued study of patents, no additional principles have been discovered.

To apply TRIZ, you would first identify the fundamental contradictions in your problem situation and then use the TRIZ contradiction table and its algorithms to map your problem against a known template of solutions to your problem's contradictions. In

**TRIZ** A methodology, a set of tools, and a knowledge base for generating innovative ideas and solutions for **KEY TERM** problems. TRIZ is based on the hypothesis that there are universal principles that form the basis for creative innovations and that we can make the process of invention more predictable by identifying, codifying, and applying these principles.

other words, you go from your specific problem to a standard problem, then from the standard solution for that problem to a specific solution for your problem.

As this work has continued, the patterns of invention also now map the progression of technologies, allowing more accurate planning, forecasting, and extensions of intellectual property filings. In another unusual twist, the basic TRIZ algorithm has been inverted and allows rapid solutions for failure analysis and failure prediction problems.

## INTRO TO **TRIZ**

**TOOLS**

TRIZ appeals more to logical, left-brained thinkers precisely because it is so logical. In my experience, it has been used principally for technical and engineering-based problems, which seems natural, since Altshuller derived TRIZ directly from the technical and engineering patent literature. To learn more, you might want to start with his book, *And Suddenly the Inventor Appeared* (Technical Innovation Center, Inc., 1992). To apply TRIZ successfully, you will probably want the assistance of a TRIZ expert; contact Jack Hipple, Innovation-TRIZ (JWH Consulting), jwhinnovator@earthlink.net.

TRIZ has a professional society, the Altshuller Institute for TRIZ Studies (*www.aitriz. org*). Every major European country, Japan, and Mexico have TRIZ associations, and most of Altshuller's books have been translated into many languages.

## Manager's Checklist for Chapter 3

☑ Remember that brainstorming must be used to "empty the box" of ideas before breaking out of the box with pattern-breaking thinking tools.

☑ Always use the sticky-note process to lead a brainstorming session. Never just stand at the flip chart with marker and ask for ideas—that is guaranteed not to work well.

☑ Commit the ladder of abstraction to memory, and use it whenever ideas are being created so that the ideas will be more specific and actionable—and useful.

☑ Constantly find ways to solicit ideas from those closest to doing the work. You may want to consider a software-based suggestion system. At the least you will want to take care of the human needs that, if ignored or neglected, will cause any suggestion system to fail.

☑ Give away all the credit for ideas and all the recognition, but be especially careful of offering rewards of money or merchandise for ideas.

# Process of Innovative Problem Solving

T he purpose of this chapter is to give an overview of the entire process of innovative problem solving. The succeeding chapters in this book will present each step in detail, so that, with some practice, you can run this process with your team.

Most people think clearly in pictures. That's why I've diagrammed a process for Bottom Line Innovation® innovative problem solving in Figure 4-1.

## Criteria for Running an Innovative Problem-Solving Workshop

Four criteria have been established that will help ensure the success of your workshop. You will want to be sure that the problem meets all four criteria, which you establish with your client early:

1. The problem must be important. It should matter significantly whether the problem gets solved or not.
2. There must be no easy or obvious solution. The "easy" solutions should have already been tried or, if the problem is a new one, there must not be any easy or obvious solutions. In addition, the boss must not have a predetermined outcome and must not be calling the session just so that his or her solution will be validated or implemented.
3. Participants *must* be committed to solving the problem and the leader must support the process by being a full participant. Partici-

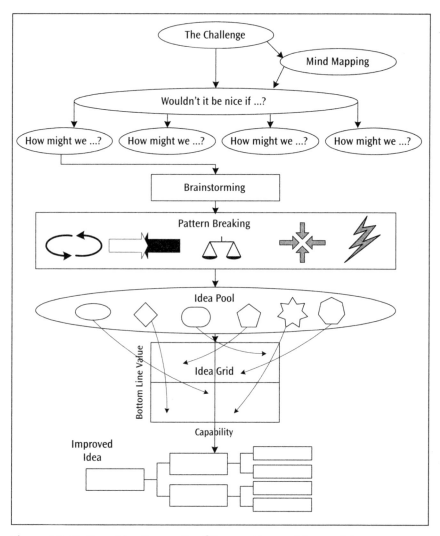

**Figure 4-1.** Bottom Line Innovation® innovative problem-solving process

pants must participate willingly; you don't want unwilling participants who would rather be somewhere else. The leader whose support is needed to implement ideas must be a full participant, not just
an interested observer, floating in and out of the session.

4. The problem should be auditable, so that you will know when
progress is being made during the implementation phase and so you
can measure and report quantitative success.

## Planning for Success

This process requires two days if run in its full expression. In today's business environment, it is very difficult to find a team that can take two full days. If the problem is important or severe enough, many times that's not an issue. Participants must take an overnight break between the brainstorming and the pattern-breaking thinking steps.

This break is critically important, because pattern-breaking thinking requires an unusually large amount of mental energy, which is in short supply after brainstorming to exhaustion. So even if you cannot take two days, it's important that the pattern-breaking thinking be done at the beginning of a day when people are refreshed.

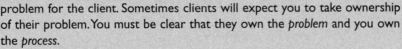

### DISTINGUISH BETWEEN PROBLEM AND PROCESS

If you are the facilitator of a team that is not your own, remember that you are now acting as a consultant, helping the client solve his or her problem. You are not solving the problem for the client. Sometimes clients will expect you to take ownership of their problem. You must be clear that they own the *problem* and you own the *process*.

If you are facilitating your own team, of course, you will own both the problem and the process and it will be harder to separate the two. It's a difficult challenge to be your own consultant. In this case, you will want to avoid the trap of manipulating the group members to think your way, selecting the problem you want selected, and then selecting the ideas you want selected.

## Roles and Responsibilities

The three roles in any innovative problem solving workshop are client, participants, and facilitator.

The *client* is responsible for the direction of the meeting: its goals, objectives, and especially any alteration that might be needed during the course of the workshop. If difficult decisions must be made about the direction, you will want to be sure that the client makes those decisions, in keeping with his or her role.

The *participants* are responsible for the outcome of the workshop. They are responsible for their own behaviors and for helping the client achieve stated objectives. They are responsible for making themselves heard and their positions considered, especially when they hold a minority view.

The *facilitator* is responsible for leading the process of the workshop and making sure that it stays on track. You will monitor progress and should point out when the discussion is off track, should that become necessary, and insist that it get back on track.

## Identify the True Client

The "true client" is the single individual who has the authority and the will to use it to assign people and resources to implement the initiatives identified by the workshop. To identify the true client, you might ask the person bringing the problem to you, "Who will have to agree with the output of this workshop before action can be taken?" If the person bringing the problem cannot do this without additional approvals, you are not yet talking with the true client.

**KEY TERM** **True Client** The person who must have to agree with the output of this workshop before action can be taken, the person with the authority and the will to use it to assign people and resources to implement the initiatives identified by the workshop.

In the sidebar below, ground rules 1 and 4 deserve special attention. The facilitator will undoubtedly have to enforce the "one conversation at a time" rule. It is very tempting for participants to engage in side conversations, typically when they have strong views and strong opinions about

**SMART MANAGING**

## GROUND RULES

You will want to display the following ground rules prominently at the beginning of any session. It is especially important when running an innovative problem-solving session.

1. One conversation at a time
2. Return from breaks promptly
3. Give your best thinking
4. No "zingers"
5. No judging ideas during idea generation
6. Build/amplify on the ideas of others
7. Have fun

a subject. The facilitator must act firmly to control this behavior because it detracts from the meeting.

The "no zinger" rule is equally important. A zinger is a very high-class put-down of some person or group. Zingers are a great energy drain on the group because energy is diverted away from problem solving and into getting even by zinging back. Dr. Scott Isaksen has shown with hard data that groups that allow zingers are 50 percent less productive than those that don't.

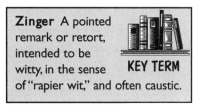

**Zinger** A pointed remark or retort, intended to be witty, in the sense of "rapier wit," and often caustic. **KEY TERM**

---

### ZINGING BY CONSENSUS

I was working with a new product development team at a major Midwest chemical company and participants representing research, marketing, and manufacturing were present. The moderator announced that it was time to hear from the research department about the progress it had made since our last meeting. The manufacturing representative said, "Well, that won't take very long, will it?"

Although it is exhilarating for the person doing the zinging to quickly and very cleverly put down a colleague, it is extremely detrimental to the innovative problem-solving process. Imagine that someone has zinged you. How do you spend your mental energy for the next 30 minutes? Of course, getting even by zinging back the original zinger.

When I announced to the group that these actions were counterproductive, they all complained that I was taking all the fun out of their meetings. They had raised zinging to an art form!

---

## Phases of the Process

There are five phases in the innovative problem-solving process. Let's review them.

### The Challenge Statement

The process of innovative problem solving (Figure 4-1) begins with the challenge statement. A challenge statement is not a statement of the problem. Rather, it is a broader statement that reflects the reason for dealing with a specific problem. You might think of a challenge statement as a floodlight illuminating an area of a dark forest. The problem statements that are created from the challenge statement are like individual trees in that portion of the forest. Chapter 5 describes how to construct a good challenge statement.

## The WIBNI Area

In Figure 4-1 the area entitled "Wouldn't it be nice if. . .?" (WIBNI) represents the process for defining the right problem, described in Chapter 6. The individual problem statements are shown below the WIBNI circle in Figure 4-1. They always begin with the phrase "How might we . . .?" In a group of about 10 participants, we usually create 10–15 individual problem statements, all of which are good. As you will see, the group must then select the "right" problem.

## Brainstorming to Exhaustion

Once the problem has been selected (Chapter 6), the task now is to "brainstorm to exhaustion," to "empty the box," to get out the "easy and obvious" ideas in preparation for thinking outside the box. A reliable process is to have participants each capture their own ideas on yellow Post-it® note paper, one idea per slip, written so that others can read it. You might want to try having participants use Sharpie® felt-tip pens so the ideas are easier to read: the writing is dark, and participants must limit the number of words. All the ideas from brainstorming are used to create the pool of ideas. Flip-chart paper is attached to the walls, and the yellow sticky notes are put onto the flip-chart paper, which becomes an idea pool. Chapter 7 describes the whole process in detail.

When brainstorming to exhaustion has been accomplished (see Chapter 7), that is usually the end of the team meeting, either because team members have run out of energy or because you have run out of time. In either case, it is pointless to take the next step, pattern-breaking thinking (Chapter 8), until there has been a break, usually overnight, so that participants will be refreshed. Pattern-breaking thinking requires a lot of mental energy, and it just doesn't work well when participants are exhausted.

## Pattern-Breaking Thinking

Now that you and your team are refreshed and have renewed energy to think, you can begin the pattern-breaking thinking process. We are all victims of our pattern thinking, as described more fully in Chapter 8. To break out of our mental box, we need a process for breaking our thinking patterns. Figure 8-1 shows that process with five tools depicted.

The importance of the facilitator role in this process cannot be overstated: this is a facilitator-dependent process. Facilitator expertise grows with practice in the same way that a pianist gets better with practice. Reading this book by itself is not enough to make you an expert, just as reading a music book by itself is not enough to make you a virtuoso musician. If you've ever studied music, you can remember how uncertain and unpolished your first attempts to play probably were. The same is true for using these techniques. The truly expert facilitators find ways to learn from each session, so they get better and better with experience.

## Selecting and Implementing the Best Ideas

Selecting and then implementing the best ideas is the final step in innovative problem solving. All too often it's not given the careful attention that it deserves. This step is described in detail in Chapter 9.

Of overriding importance is the principle of making idea selections based on agreed-on criteria, using one at a time (staged criteria). You will want to review the criteria listed in Chapter 9 and confirm that they are right for your organization and circumstance; if they are not, change them with full and open discussion with your team. For example, the criteria for selecting a good idea at a nonprofit organization will not be the same criteria shown in Chapter 9 for a company in business to make a profit.

Once the ideas have been selected, there will be 85 percent of the original ideas remaining in the idea pool. Give participants the opportunity to select any yet unselected idea that strongly appeals to them and commit to taking the next step to decide if the idea merits full scale-up. This "side step" is described in Chapter 9.

We have presented five worksheets in the Appendix that are to be reproduced and used during the idea implementation steps. Once these have been completed for the very best ideas, you will want to set up an audit schedule so that you can know the progress being made and where to shift resources if needed.

# Example of Success: An International Publisher

Samantha Stead, a manager at a major international publisher, and Brian Dorval of Creative Problem Solving Group-Buffalo are both committed, highly skilled, and experienced facilitators. They have described some of the results of using innovative problem-solving processes with a major international publishing and direct marketing company ("New Product Development: Changing the Rules of the Game," *CPSB's Communique,* Vol. 10, 2000, pp. 1-3).

The publishing company sells direct to consumers on a subscription basis. Its products include books, audio books, music, collectible porcelain, china, and glassware, and the company has a reputation for very high quality. During the five-plus years of using innovative problem-solving processes, sessions have been devoted to new products and marketing concepts, effective teamwork and leadership behavior, evaluation and strengthening of products, establishment of personal training and development needs, financial planning and accounting systems, and others.

## Product Development

Before innovative problem solving, the process worked this way: the product came first with a good idea, it was developed, customers liked it, it was marketed, but it did *not* deliver the expected results. After using innovative problem solving, the right problem was defined before the solutions were created, by understanding global trends, defining market opportunities, establishing customer needs, and developing products to meet those needs. The results exceeded expectations.

Before innovative problem solving, products were developed locally without knowledge of the real customer need, typically at a cost of $40,000 per product to get to the first round of decision making. After using innovative problem solving, global development was done based on global customer needs—all at a cost of $13,000 to reach the second round of decision making. With nine products in the pipeline, the new process saved more than $250,000 over the old process.

## Retaining Subscription Customers

Before innovative problem solving, the company retained only 3 percent of the customers who called to cancel. Many improvements were tried, but to no avail. There were inherent discontinuities in expectations for the customer service staff, such as "Answer as many calls as possible but at the same time spend time retaining customers." Morale and motivation among the customer service employees was poor.

Using innovative problem solving enabled a clear understanding of the issues and enabled effective action. The customer service staff was encouraged to own the issues and take responsibility for fixing what was within their power. As a result, the company was able to retain 68 percent of customers who called to cancel, representing an increase in revenue of $1.6 million per year.

# Example of Success: Whirlpool Corporation

Whirlpool Corporation is known for its innovative approach consistently supported by top leadership throughout the organization. Theirs is a highly structured innovation process that they practice with discipline, making sure they have the voice of the customer as the driver. They insist that every innovation be aimed squarely at solving a customer need.

Todd Starr, brand director for Gladiator® GarageWorks, has recounted the innovations that led to the new GarageWorks product category far from the company's core business. In 2000, some 30-plus people were trained in the Whirlpool formal innovation process, and then they were to roll out the tools to the broader organization. From one of their innovative problem-solving workshops came the idea of appliances for the garage. Their consumer studies revealed that the garage is considered the man's room and, sadly, is sometimes known as the "junk drawer of the home." This represented a giant departure in the traditional marketing approach at Whirlpool: appliances are generally purchased by women, but appliances for the garage would be purchased by men. The Gladiator® brand was launched in 2003, with distribution through Sears, Lowe's, and high-end garage decorators and on a Web site (*www.gladiatorgw.com*).

## Characteristics of the Climate

Starr explained the major characteristics of the climate at Whirlpool that helped make this project so successful.

1. Resources were dedicated to the Appliances for the Garage team. It's impossible to continue with a regular job and do innovation like this

in your spare time. Although money was scarce, the team was resourced to win.

2. The team was treated like internal entrepreneurs (*intrepreneurs*, to use a term coined by Gifford Pinchot in his article, "Intra-Corporate Entrepreneurship," 1978) within Whirlpool Corporation. Unlike entrepreneurs working on their own, the team members had the luxury of a secure paycheck every month, so they could focus on developing and commercializing the Gladiator® brand without having to worry about paying their bills.

3. The team members were encouraged to be bold and different; company leaders gave them license to stretch beyond normal limits. The product line needed an appearance and a name that conveyed masculinity, quite a departure from traditional Whirlpool marketing. The Gladiator name was reinforced by the use of industrial metal surfaces that give a strong masculine image. The sales channel needed to be different, so they decided to sell direct to consumers from a Web site as well as through Lowe's and Sears. Even though only 15 percent of sales come through the Web site, a much larger percentage of profit has resulted.

4. Every team member was passionate about the Appliances for the Garage. Todd Starr commented that the passion for the project was

---

**FOR EXAMPLE**

### INNOVATION ON THE CHEAP

Even though the team was funded, it was a shoestring budget that called on the best creative thinking from the group to get the job done at a lower cost. To test consumer acceptance early and at low cost, the summer intern gave $5 rolls of postage stamps as thank-you gifts to people agreed to be interviewed at one of the shopping malls. When the team needed a video, which was going to cost many thousands of dollars, it arranged to trade some Gladiator® products and KitchenAid® mixers to lower the price. When it needed more research on garages, it worked with the corporate anthropologist and hired a graduate student in anthropology to do the interviews, which led to deep consumer insights that helped guide the project. When the team needed a product designer and their staff members were too busy to help, it engaged a young man whom one team member knew at a nearby company. That person now leads the design for the Maytag brand.

critical to help keep the team moving ahead, despite occasional killer phrases from naysayers.

When Whirlpool wanted to continue to grow Gladiator® by selling more through home improvement stores, the Gladiator® product line didn't fit the need of the home improvement store customers, which is to buy a product, take it home, and begin using it over the weekend. The Gladiator® products were assembled and shipped in brown boxes like appliances. The products wouldn't fit into cars, and they took up too much space in the stores. The Gladiator® line needed a complete over-haul. The components were redesigned for do-it-yourself assembly, eight-foot cabinet sections were reduced to four feet to fit into cars, and the components were shipped in white boxes with pictures of assembly and use, since most home improvement stores have few sales associates to help. Innovation in product design, with the needs of this new marketing outlet and these new customers in mind, was the key to success.

---

### APPLYING INNOVATION TO APPLIANCES

FOR EXAMPLE

Some examples of innovation successes at Whirlpool include the first icemaker that's part of the refrigerator door, an ice bin that can be lifted out easily, and a dispenser that delivers cold water twice as fast as any other brand. Also, some 10 years ago their consumer studies made them aware of a big productivity issue with their washers and dryers. The conventional top-loading washer could wash a lot faster than the dryer could dry, so a person doing multiple laundry loads always had to wait for the dryer to catch up with the washer. This problem was solved by creating a front-loading washer that with not only greater capacity but also a spin-dry speed almost twice that of the conventional top-loading washers. The clothes contain less moisture as they leave the washer, so the dryer uses much less energy and can keep up with the washer.

---

# Example of Success: United Way

Innovation requires faith and patience, especially on the part of leaders. This is a story of how faith and patience for an innovative program at United Way are paying off.

Bradford Frost, Brand Strategist for United Way for Southeastern Michigan (UWSEM), describes its Reading Village innovation, which not only promises to provide tremendous community value but also helped create an internal competency for innovation, which is evolving and being used repeatedly on other community projects.

In 2005, United Way decided to move away from its traditional fundraising model to a more hands-on community problem-solving model. At the same time, in March 2005, UWSEM was formed when United Way Community Services in Detroit and United Way of Oakland County in Pontiac joined together to better serve the three-county region. The new United Way identified the core issues facing the community as education, financial stability, and basic needs.

For its initial innovation process, UWSEM decided to focus on the education needs of the community, where 13 percent of the third-grade children in southeastern Michigan, or roughly 7,000, were reading below grade level. Strongly supported by their leaders without the pressure of an artificial deadline, the group of employees and key volunteers, headed by a retired consultant from Accenture, spent the first six months meeting every other week for two hours to understand the causes of this reading deficiency, the methods used to teach reading, and the drivers of literacy success.

The Reading Village task force was a cross-functional team composed of a retired consultant, a brand strategist, an early childhood development specialist, a retired speech pathologist, a university researcher, a communications specialist, and a United Way fundraiser. Their goal was to have all children in the tri-county area reading at grade level by third grade. All team members had other functional responsibilities, which they continued as they volunteered for this team.

In six months of part-time work, the team developed a distinct set of drivers, which were used to help design the Reading Village project. The strongest predictors that a child will not be ready in first grade are low birth weight, low-income household, and single mother. When all three risk factors are present, the team found there's almost no chance that the child would be ready by first grade. With further work they also found that three elements are present when children read at grade level: being read to 20 to 30 minutes per day by someone with the time and the skills, using age-appropriate books, and a committed parent.

The team created an opportunity for the Reading Navigator, a person with the skills and time willing to volunteer to help create a literacy-rich home environment for the child and his or her family. This includes making sure someone reads to the children and that the parent has the skills and know-how to help with the child's educational development.

A core component of the Reading Village program is Internet-based support, but many in this demographic did not have a computer. An innovation was to understand how families could have access to the Internet to take advantage of these resources. The team found that the most consistent tool available to this demographic was the cell phone. UWSEM is offering some families in the pilot phase the use of a *smartphone*, provided the parent commits to the three core supports (reading to the child 20-30 minutes per day, using age-appropriate books, and being a committed parent). The smartphone allows access to a Web site developed for participating children and parents and to a social network created for families in the Reading Village program.

> **DON'T EXPECT TOO MUCH TOO SOON**
>
> **CAUTION**
>
> Many managers have little faith or patience with innovation, which causes them to expect results too quickly after an initiative begins. They're like farmers who plant corn and then, rather than wait for time and nature to produce a harvest, they go "dig up the seeds to see if the roots are growing"—which of course kills the plants. Innovation takes time, usually more than anticipated. The leaders at UWSEM had both faith and patience and gave innovation a chance to take hold.

---

**WHAT MADE THE PROCESS OF INNOVATION WORK?**    *TRICKS OF THE TRADE*

Two elements stand out as most important in the creation and development of the Reading Village program.

1. Strong support from leaders with faith in the people and the program and the patience to see it through were crucial to success. Burdensome artificial deadlines would have caused the team to stop with the first good ideas and thus miss some of the more innovative ideas.
2. The team members developed a trust to co-create, which greatly enabled the result. Members had empathy and confidence in each other's competence, contributions, and the process. This was a truly open endeavor.

In August 2008 the prototype stage began with three Reading Navigators and eight families. Although initial results from the pilot are just now becoming available, it is clear that attention by parents is increasing, and reading is improving. In its second year, the program is being expanded to 25 Reading Navigators and 60 families.

# Attributes of Successful Facilitators of Innovation

In case you are considering having several people trained to facilitate innovative problem-solving sessions, we have developed a list of attributes that are strongly correlated with success in that role.

1. **Strong personal desire.** The person is probably not going to be assigned as a full-time facilitator; facilitating will require doing additional work, so it helps if he or she really wants to do it.

2. **Good interpersonal skills.** The facilitator must not irritate the participants. In one of my early sessions, one of the facilitators got into a shouting match with a participant—who turned out to be the sponsor of the entire session. (The facilitator didn't know it.) Digging deeper, I found that this facilitator had a history of poor interpersonal relations in her other assignments. We were unable to continue to use her.

3. **High energy and enthusiasm.** This is particularly important if the group is composed of high-talent introverts who dislike speaking up (the biggest challenge for a facilitator).

4. **Extroverted behavior.** The facilitator is putting on a show and it helps if he or she enjoys it. We have trained some high-talent introverts in this process, only to find that they don't enjoy it and therefore never use it.

5. **"Out of the box" (right-brained) thinking.** In dead times, when participants are generating no ideas, the facilitator must act as a "spark plug" by suggesting specific ideas. Right-brained thinkers have a much easier time doing this than left-brained thinkers.

6. **Experience facilitating groups.** Nothing builds confidence more than experience. Although it's not required, the person preparing to facilitate may wish to take a facilitator training course.

# Manager's Checklist for Chapter 4

☑ Make sure that any innovative problem-solving session meets the four criteria:
- ■ The problem must be important.
- ■ There must be no easy or obvious solution.
- ■ Participants must be committed to solving the problem, and the leader must support the process by being a full participant.
- ■ The problem should be auditable.

☑ Remember the roles and responsibilities of the client, the participants, and the facilitator.

☑ Always honor the desire of a participant to personally commit to an idea he or she really wants to champion. It's probably that individual's own idea, and if it can be made to work, he or she is the best one to make it happen.

☑ Be sure that candidates for facilitator training possess the personal attributes that strongly correlate with success in that role.

☑ Always remind yourself and your sponsors that faith and patience are required for innovation to take hold and deliver results. Don't "dig up the seeds to see if the roots are growing."

# Developing a Challenge Statement

The *challenge statement* starts everything. It is a broad statement of the reason for team members to gather to deal with an issue or to solve a problem. The challenge statement is not the problem statement. Rather, it identifies the challenge by shining a floodlight on part of the dark forest of potential problems. It focuses our thinking and is the foundation for defining the real problem to be solved.

When a team meets for problem solving, members may think they understand the problem well and don't need to discuss it much. Nothing could be further from the truth. It is a mistake to assume we know what the problem is. Some authorities call this frame of mind *mental fixedness*, *mental set*, or *functional fixedness*, when we are so very sure of ourselves.

That's why the challenge statement is so important—it helps us overcome mental fixedness and it gets everyone on the same page with the same goal in mind. It unifies team members around a commonly understood challenge that will lead them to the right problem. You'll find that there are many "right problems," so choosing the best one to work on is an issue unto itself, to be discussed later.

## Understand the Situation

It is imperative that everyone understand the current situation. Therefore, you will want to spend as much time as necessary to ensure that participants in any problem-solving session are totally up-to-date on the current situation.

Let's assume that you own a small computer business in a college town. Part of your situation is that PC-Max, a big-box store, is planning to build in your area, and you fear that you will lose business to it unless you do something innovative to maintain or even grow your own business.

You start by establishing your situation.

*Elements of Our Situation*

1. We believe that the customer is #1.
2. We have an on-site repair department.
3. Repairs are done within three days.
4. We serve a number of widely different market segments.
5. We sell brand-name and clone PCs and software.

> **Challenge Statement** A broad statement of the reason for dealing with an issue or solving a problem. **KEY TERM**
>
> A challenge statement is not a problem statement. A challenge statement identifies an issue or a problem that needs attention or consideration and indicates why it is a challenge and how it relates to the future state.
>
> A challenge statement focuses thinking and forms the foundation for defining the problem to be solved. It helps problem-solving teams dispel assumptions and preconceptions they might have about the problem and gets all team members onto the same page with the same goal in mind.

## Craft the Challenge Statement

Crafting a challenge statement requires practice. There are a few rules you must observe:

1. Challenge statements are always written in the following format: "WE MUST _____, SO THAT_____."

To continue with the case study of the computer store, you might write: "WE MUST find ways to compete effectively with the big-box stores SO THAT we can remain profitable and continue growing."

2. The challenge statement must contain only one challenge. You must never combine two or more challenges into one. Use of the word "and" is a strong tipoff that you have violated this rule.

*Bad:* "WE MUST find ways to compete effectively with the big-box stores *and* Internet competitors SO THAT we can remain profitable and continue growing."

3. The challenge statement must contain no hint of a possible solution. Your challenge statement should contain no suggestion of how you plan to go about it. Use of the word "by" is a strong tipoff that you have violated this rule.

*Bad:* "WE MUST find ways to compete effectively with the big-box stores *by* increasing our marketing effort SO THAT we can remain profitable and continue growing."

As you help your team develop a proper challenge statement, think about its degree of abstraction. (Remember the ladder of abstraction from Chapter 3.) The more general and abstract the statement, the less useful it will probably turn out to be. On the other hand, if the challenge statement is extremely specific, its focus will be too narrow and it will presuppose a solution.

One way to make your challenge statement more specific is to make the "WE MUST" section the "SO THAT" section of a new statement and create a new "WE MUST" section. In our case study, we could make the original challenge statement ("WE MUST find ways to compete effectively with the big-box stores SO THAT we can remain profitable and continue growing") more specific in the following way: "WE MUST _____ SO THAT we can find ways to compete effectively with the big-box stores." Now, of course, we need to fill in the "WE MUST" part.

> **SOLVE THE CAUSE, NOT THE EFFECTS**
>
> **FOR EXAMPLE**  A health insurance company was dealing with the issue of extremely high training costs for its customer telephone call center. Turnover was high, and training of new hires required six to eight weeks before they were allowed to take customer calls. During the discussion to develop the challenge statement, the team members realized that the problem was not training costs and time, but turnover. As a result, their challenge statement became "WE MUST find ways to reduce turnover in the call center SO THAT training costs will be reduced."

There are a number of right ways to do this, and you will need to guide the discussion. For example, you might say, "WE MUST understand what our customers truly want SO THAT we can find ways to compete effectively with the big-box stores." You can see that this challenge statement is more specific and is potentially more useful. It is more directive, but not so focused that it allows only one direction in thinking. We will use this challenge statement as we continue the case study through idea generation and selection and implementation.

## Clarify What You Really Want—The Four Quadrants

Most of the time, our clients ask us to help them grow the business. They are unsure about how to do it. All they know is the growth rate is low and profits are down. One of the things we use to help them clarify what they really want is the Market–Technology Matrix shown in Figure 5-1.

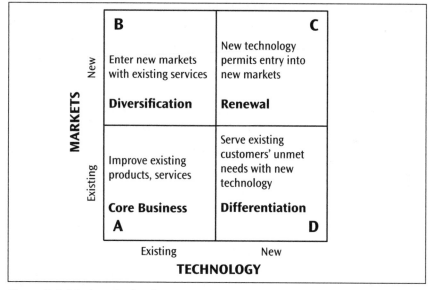

**Figure 5-1.** Market–Technology Matrix

The horizontal axis is labeled "Technology: Existing → New" (or "Products: Existing → New"), and the vertical axis is labeled "Markets: Existing → New." Our core business is found in the lower left quadrant: we sell existing technology (products) in existing markets. This is the *core* quadrant. Focus on this quadrant must continue so that the business can continue on a day-to-day basis. In the upper left quadrant is *diversification*. It is here that we sell existing technology (products) in new markets. An example might be expanding the sales of dog food normally sold in chain pet stores into upscale grocery stores. In the lower right quadrant is *differentiation*: we create new technology (products) to serve existing markets in a better way. Using the dog food example, we might develop a line of organic dog food products commanding a premium price, therefore differentiating us from our nearest competitor. In the upper right quadrant is *renewal,* in which new technology allows our entry into new markets.

Successful organizations over time will move toward the renewal quadrant. However, most do not move directly from the core quadrant to the renewal quadrant at once; they usually go through the differentiation or the diversification quadrant first.

## Business Risk and Innovation Potential

In moving from the core quadrant of the Market–Technology Matrix of Figure 5-1 into any of the other quadrants, the business risk is inversely proportional to the level of innovation. The lowest-risk move is to simply expand business in the core quadrant, but of course this move has the lowest possibility of innovation. The next lowest risk is to move from the core quadrant into the diversification quadrant, putting existing technology (products) into new markets. The next lowest risk is to move from the core into the differentiation quadrant, putting new technology (products) into existing markets. The greatest risk occurs in moving from the core quadrant to the renewal quadrant in one step, because both technology and markets change at the same time, but of course innovation potential is highest.

Here's a way to help your organization clarify what it really wants. While developing the challenge statement, engage leaders in a discussion of the Market–Technology Matrix, and establish which direction they would like to move. "Beginning in the core quadrant, should growth be into new markets with our existing products and technology or should it be into existing markets with new products and technology that differentiate us from the competition?"

I know the answer already: they always say they want both. Unfortunately, the things you must do to move into the diversification quadrant are not the things you must do to move into the differentiation quadrant. Of course, that means that the challenge statement must be focused on one or the other—it's a huge mistake to combine both directions into a single challenge statement. These really are two challenges and you should *not* deal with both in the same workshop. First, the people who can contribute most to moving into the diversification quadrant are probably not the same people who can contribute the most to moving into the differentiation quadrant. Second, combining two dissimilar challenges into one is programmed to fail.

You will need to be firm and insist on focusing on only one challenge in the first workshop. You might suggest a second workshop to follow up with the other challenge.

It's a good idea to wait until the challenge statement has been agreed upon before deciding which specific individuals to invite to the problem-solving workshop. This way you will be able to invite the right people with the right expertise to deal effectively with the challenge area.

> **ONLY ONE DIRECTION**
>
>
> **CAUTION**
>
> Focus the challenge statement on only one direction of movement—either diversification or differentiation. Moving in both directions generally involves two groups of people and requires two types of strategies and tactics.

---

> **GET THE CHALLENGE STATEMENT RIGHT**          **SMART**
>
> **MANAGING**
>
> It takes practice to achieve a reasonable level of abstraction as you craft challenge statements. If you find during your problem-solving session that the challenge statement is either too general or too specific, immediately engage your team in helping you find the right level of abstraction by writing a number of new statements.
>
> Crafting the right challenge statement may even take an hour or so, but it's worth the investment of time because this sets the stage for defining the problem. The American Indians have a wonderful saying that applies here: "If you realize you are riding a dead horse, dismount!"

## Manager's Checklist for Chapter 5

☑ Always write challenge statements in the form, "WE MUST _____, SO THAT _____" and fill in the blanks.

☑ Be sure that your challenge statement contains only one challenge and no hint of a path to a solution.

☑ When you believe you have a workable challenge statement, write a new one with the "SO THAT" portion becoming the "WE MUST" section and creating a new "WE MUST" section.

☑ If the team challenge is one of business growth, use the Market–Technology Matrix in a discussion with your leaders so that you understand clearly the direction of intended growth. This enables you to be on target with your team as you develop the challenge statement.

☑ Have each of your team members individually draft five challenge statements reflecting the direction from the Market–Technology Matrix. In a team meeting, discuss and modify them all to arrive at the one the team will use as it solves the problem. Usually the selected challenge statement is a combination of several.

# Defining the Right Problem

Now that you have an acceptable challenge statement, the time has come to identify and then select the best problem statement that is hiding under the challenge statement. There will be 10 to 15 "right problems," all of which have the challenge statement as their foundation. However, using our criteria for selection, you'll easily recognize the two or three "best problems" that are more likely to produce great ideas about meeting the stated challenge.

## WIBNI—The Self-Seeking Process

To start working toward "best problems" to target and defining the right problem, one method is to think in terms of wishing—"Wouldn't it be nice if . . . ?" (WIBNI). Figure 6-1 illustrates the WIBNI process. It is truly a self-seeking process because we begin with the end in mind.

We start with the current situation, on the left of the figure. I picture it as a thundercloud, since things aren't quite so perfect. If everyone on the team is not fully up to speed, you should have someone describe the situation that leads us to want to be more innovative. This explanation does not have to be long, but it should be detailed enough so that everyone understands where we are. It is a time for question and answer. Everyone should ask questions and get answers. This process should continue until there are no more questions.

SMART
MANAGING

**BEGIN BY IMAGINING**

Keep in mind the following words, which summarize the process of creation:

"Imagination is the beginning of creation. You imagine what you desire, you will what you imagine and at last you create what you will."

—George Bernard Shaw (1856-1950)

Let's return to the challenge statement developed in our case study in Chapter 5: "WE MUST understand what our customers truly want SO THAT we can find ways to compete effectively with the big-box stores."

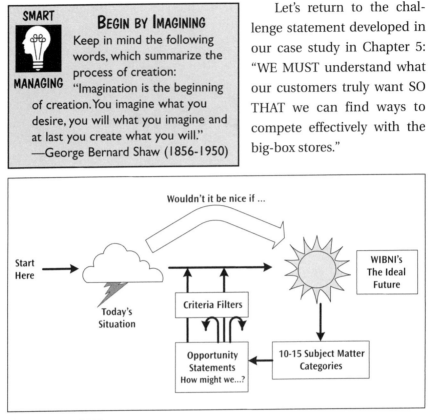

**Figure 6-1.** WIBNI process

Next, using sticky notes, everyone should write down 10 statements that begin with "Wouldn't it be nice if …" (WIBNI), putting each statement on a separate note. It is critical that the WIBNI statements be written on the "WE MUST" section of the challenge statement ("WE MUST understand what our customers truly want"); WIBNI statements written on the "SO THAT" section give nothing of value, since that section represents the outcome. An example: "WIBNI our customers knew what they wanted."

Once the team members have all written out 10 WIBNI statements, the facilitator (it might be you or someone you appoint) leads the process of categorizing the WIBNI statements into subject categories. There are a number ways of doing this. My preference is for the facilitator to ask for one WIBNI from one participant, read it aloud, and ask the group to help decide how to categorize the WIBNI. Write the subject category on a sticky note and place it on a flip chart. Stick the WIBNI below the category label. Then, ask who else has a WIBNI that falls into the same category. Place any WIBNIs that belong in that category below the category label.

This is a reiterative process. Ask for another WIBNI, create its subject category, and place the appropriate WIBNIs under it. Continue until all WIBNIs have been handled.

Proper placement of WIBNIs is not nearly so important as the quality of the subject categories. Identifying the right subject categories is critically important, because the problem statements will come directly from these category headings.

Figure 6-2 shows the subject categories for the case study with individual WIBNI statements listed underneath each.

## Conversion to Problem Statements

Now that all the subject categories have been decided, it's time to convert them into *problem statements*, sometimes called *opportunity statements*. This is an easy step: it consists simply of writing "How might we …" plus an appropriate verb or phrase and then the category name. The choice of the verb is also very important, because it leads team members to think of the action to be taken. For example, "How might we reduce employee turnover?" is quite different from "How might we understand employee turnover?" As team leader you'll want to be sure that the verbs are on target for the challenge.

---

### RULES FOR PROBLEM STATEMENTS

TRICKS OF THE TRADE

The rules for problem statements are very similar to the rules for challenge statements:

1. One problem per problem statement. Resist the temptation to join two problem statements. The tip-off is the word "and": e.g., "How might we reduce turnover *and* improve employee morale in our call center?" It's much more effective to create two problem statements.
2. Refrain from saying how you will solve the problem. The tip-off is the word "by": e.g., "How might we reduce our costs *by* consolidating suppliers?"

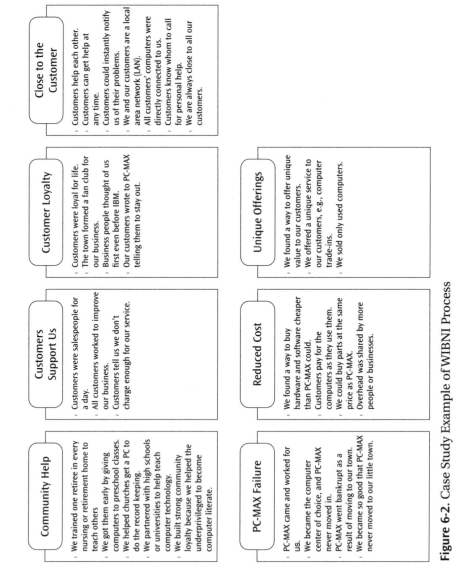

**Community Help**

- We trained one retiree in every nursing or retirement home to teach others
- We got them early by giving computers to preschool classes.
- We helped churches get a PC to do the record keeping.
- We partnered with high schools or universities to help teach computer technology.
- We built strong community loyalty because we helped the underprivileged to become computer literate.

**Customers Support Us**

- Customers were salespeople for a day.
- All customers worked to improve our business.
- Customers tell us we don't charge enough for our service.

**Customer Loyalty**

- Customers were loyal for life.
- The town formed a fan club for our business.
- Business people thought of us first even before IBM.
- Our customers wrote to PC-MAX telling them to stay out.

**Close to the Customer**

- Customers help each other.
- Customers can get help at any time.
- Customers could instantly notify us of their problems.
- We and our customers are a local area network (LAN).
- All customers' computers were directly connected to us.
- Customers know whom to call for personal help.
- We are always close to all our customers.

**PC-MAX Failure**

- PC-MAX came and worked for us.
- We became the computer center of choice, and PC-MAX never moved in.
- PC-MAX went bankrupt as a result of moving to our town.
- We became so good that PC-MAX never moved to our little town.

**Reduced Cost**

- We found a way to buy hardware and software cheaper than PC-MAX could.
- Customers pay for the computers as they use them.
- We could buy parts at the same price as PC-MAX.
- Overhead was shared by more people or businesses.

**Unique Offerings**

- We found a way to offer unique value to our customers.
- We offered a unique service to our customers, e.g., computer trade-ins.
- We sold only used computers.

**Figure 6-2.** Case Study Example of WIBNI Process

When all the problem statements have been correctly written, the time has come to select the best one and create innovative ideas for solving it. Continuing with our case study, converting the subject categories into problem statements, we get the following results:

1. How might we help the community?
2. How might we get our customers to support us?
3. How might we guarantee customer loyalty?
4. How might we get close to the customer?
5. How might we ensure big-box failure?
6. How might we reduce our costs?
7. How might we provide unique offerings?

## The Magic of Criteria in the Selection Process

We all make choices every day. Every time we make a choice in private or in public, we do so with a set of internally held criteria that most often we never disclose. In our process of selecting a problem statement, we insist that agreed-upon criteria be used as we make choices. That way, there are no hidden agendas and all team members make their selection based on the same set of criteria. This use of established criteria almost ensures uniformity in agreement about what the most important problems are and it

---

**MAKE THE DECISION IN ADVANCE**

Please select the most important of the following four items:

1. Unexpected $10,000 bonus
2. Free vacation for you and your partner or spouse to Hawaii in the middle of winter
3. Vanilla ice cream cone
4. Good health

If you happen to be a functional adult, you undoubtedly have selected item 4, good health. However, if I made the same choice available to a four-year-old child, he or she would undoubtedly select the ice cream cone. Your criterion was probably long-term benefit whereas the child's criterion was probably short-term payoff.

We cannot expect a group of individuals to all have the same criteria for any decision. That's why it's smart to agree in advance on criteria for making decisions. It also speeds up the decision process and minimizes disagreements.

minimizes disputes. People are on the same wavelength about the most important problems.

In business meetings when those gathered must make hard choices about how to allocate limited resources, each party argues from his or her own criteria. A better process to gain consensus on the set of criteria that everyone will use is to make tough choices, prioritize them, and write them prominently on a flip chart. Then, ask each participant to decide for himself or herself which of the problem statements are more likely to meet the criteria. After the selection is finally made, you may want to check back to see how well the criteria were observed.

## Expected Criteria in For-Profit Companies

We have consistently found that the following criteria are used for problem selection in companies in business to make a profit.

1. The problem statement deals with an absolute "must-have." It might be an issue mandated by a governmental agency, a critical safety-related issue, or some critical business issue that cannot be ignored. If this is the case, this problem statement will be selected and carried forward through implementation, by definition. If there are no "absolute must-haves," then begin with criterion #2.
2. The problem statement will likely be highly effective in meeting the challenge statement.
3. The team has the power and authority to implement or influence actions in this area.
4. Solving the problem will put the company ahead of the competition.

## Passionate Campaign Speeches Help Create Consensus

After the group members have agreed on the criteria to be used, invite participants to make an impassioned campaign speech in support of their favorite problem statement. This is an important step, because individual participants will have a viewpoint that perhaps no one else has considered before and good speeches can sway votes. It's probably wise for the team leader to withhold expressing an opinion until the end, so as not to influence what others might say.

---

### Don't Skip the Speeches

Allowing campaign speeches supporting favorite problem statements is a critically important step, because it gives everyone a voice and that's the best way to achieve team consensus. Consensus does not mean 100 percent agreement. Consensus means that every team member will support the decision made by the team, even if it is not the decision he or she would have made.

You can always tell when true consensus is reached by how strongly all team members continue to voice support for the team position, especially when they are away from others on the team. Members do not necessarily expect the team to adopt their point of view; they simply want to have their positions thoughtfully and honestly considered before decisions are made. When team members have had a fair hearing, they are much more willing to support the decision of the team.

## Selecting the Right Problem

Once the campaign speeches are finished and there are no more questions you will want to move quickly to voting. This can be done in various ways—from a show of hands to private written ballots.

If there is a clear winner in the vote, copy the problem statement on a fresh sheet of flip chart paper, and get ready for the next step in the next chapter. If, however, two or three problem statements get an equal number of votes, you will need to decide which one to select. One way is to break the tie by giving each team member another sticky dot of a different color to cast. Another way out of the deadlock is simply to have the senior member of management in the room make the decision; he or she should also provide an explanation.

In our case study, there were eight participants, each of whom received two sticky

### Stick with Simplicity

We recommend *dot voting*. Buy colored sticky dots from an office supply store. Give each participant no more than three sticky dots, so that there will be a forced choice. If you make the mistake of giving as many dots as there are problem statements, it will be harder to discern the clear winner. Invite team members to get out of their seats and affix their voting dots to the problem statements written on flip chart paper on the wall. The team leader will probably want to go last, so as not to influence the voting. When all the dots have been affixed, simply add the number of dots for each problem statement.

dots with which to vote. Here's the way it turned out:

| Problem Statement | Number of Votes |
| --- | --- |
| 1, How might we help the community? | 0 |
| 2. How might we get our customers to support us? | 0 |
| 3. How might we guarantee customer loyalty? | 2 |
| 4. How might we get close to the customer? | 8 |
| 5. How might we ensure big-box failure? | 0 |
| 6. How might we reduce our costs? | 2 |
| 7. How might we provide unique offerings? | 4 |
| Total = | 16 |

The clear winner is problem #4, "How might we get close to the customer?"

This problem will be carried forward to the next chapters on idea generation, selection, and implementation.

## Manager's Checklist for Chapter 6

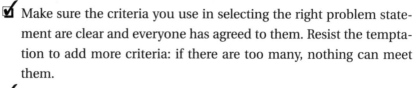 Make sure everyone understands the current situation before you begin the WIBNI process for defining the right problem.

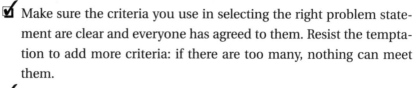 Carefully place the WIBNI statements of ideal outcome into subject matter categories. Keep in mind that these subject categories will be converted into problem statements, so how these categories are written is critical. Too general a category will provide no direction; yet too specific a category will force thinking down a single pathway. Feel free to modify the names of categories as you move along, if it makes sense to do so.

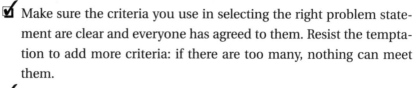 Make sure the criteria you use in selecting the right problem statement are clear and everyone has agreed to them. Resist the temptation to add more criteria: if there are too many, nothing can meet them.

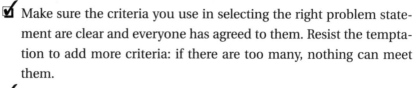 When the right problem has been selected, verify it with the sponsor or client before proceeding. This is a question of direction, and that is the responsibility of the sponsor or client.

# Brainstorming to
# Empty the Box

I n this chapter you will learn the process of using sticky notes to "empty the box" of ideas by brainstorming to exhaustion. Give this process a try just once, and you will never go back to the old way of writing the ideas on a flip chart again.

As described in Chapter 3, we have found overwhelming evidence that allowing individuals to think and record their ideas before sharing them greatly increases the quantity and avoids groupthink, in which everyone thinks down the same path because it is under discussion. That's why, in the following activity, we ask that participants first write their ideas silently before sharing. They then build on the ideas of others by pairing up to share their ideas and generate more.

Following through with the case study from Chapter 6, the selected problem statement was "How might we get close to the customer?" This problem statement should be clearly copied onto a flip chart for all to see.

In addition, you should also have a flip chart showing the ladder of abstraction (see Chapter 3) and explain again that you're looking for ideas at the bottom of the ladder, which are more detailed, and not at the top of the ladder, which are more conceptual. In my experience, even with this instruction, people will still continue to give you conceptual statements that are not useful. This is because creating conceptual ideas is easy; it's much more difficult to create specific and actionable ideas.

**WORK THROUGH AN EXAMPLE**

To save time and energy and reduce frustration, you may want to do a short group exercise using the ladder of abstraction and "how?" questions. If you choose an example with which participants are likely to be familiar, it should be easier to involve them and warm them up for working with the selected problem statement.

You could use for your example a situation in which a group of people have been meeting and are hungry: "We must agree on eating something so that we will be satisfied and able to continue this meeting." Offer a few conceptual ideas as starters and then use "how?" questions to invite ideas that move down the ladder of abstraction.

Explain that the next step is to develop specific and actionable ideas to solve this problem. To do that, we first must empty the box with brainstorming.

## The Process

As described in Chapter 3, the process is to use 3" x 3" Post-it® notes. Every participant should have a notepad. Your instructions are to have each work independently and silently as they write their 10 ideas about how they would solve the problem if it were their only job. You will want to check the ideas being written, making sure that they are specific enough.

When the participants have created their quota of 10 ideas each, the next step is to have each participant share with the person sitting to the left or the right. The objective is for the two to build on each other's ideas. Each pair of participants should create five new ideas, which they capture on sticky notes.

Once they have generated and captured five ideas, each two participants step to the board, read their ideas aloud, and place them on flip chart paper attached to the wall (the *idea pool*). In this way all the members of the group get to hear all the ideas. There will be many duplicate ideas. It's good practice to group the ideas so that like ideas are placed at about the same location on the flip chart paper.

Using the case study as an example, here are some of the brainstormed ideas:

**PUSH IDEAS DOWN THE LADDER OF ABSTRACTION**

A participant might write a conceptual idea that reads, "Communicate more." You will want to point out that it's a good beginning, but you need more detail than that: the idea must answer the "how?" question in order to be more specific and actionable and useful. You will want to engage the participant in answering the "how?" question so others can learn from this experience. The idea might become "Employees ask every customer what problems or questions they have" or "Start a customer newsletter and have customers write a column every month." These ideas are specific and more actionable and a lot more useful than the conceptual idea. These ideas would get captured on sticky notes.

1. Phone customers after the sale to ensure satisfaction.
2. Have a special phone line dedicated for help calls.
3. Offer in-home help with new systems.
4. Create a list of customers who offered to tutor other customers.
5. Send customers birthday cards.
6. Provide a free library of instructional videos about software to customers.
7. Provide evening tutorial sessions for customers on popular software.
8. Maintain a customer list with every component purchased so we know what they've got when they call.
9. Assign every customer his or her own personal contact person at the store, including the employee's cell phone number.
10. Have every employee visit one major customer each week.

These brainstormed ideas are typical. They are new and useful, but easily copied by any competitor and are not very innovative. Yet, many organizations never do nearly as good a job as they could with brainstorming, and in many cases this process of emptying the box might be all that's needed.

I have found that if a company has never dealt with a problem effectively, the brainstormed ideas are often good enough and represent the "low-hanging fruit" that must be picked first. These ideas are usually easier to implement and could be all that's needed as a first cut.

However, if the problem has been the subject of a number of attempts, brainstorming will only rehash what has already been considered before and there generally won't be very much that is really new. That's when pattern-breaking thinking, as described in Chapter 8, becomes critically important to innovation.

One pass through this idea-generating process usually empties the box for most people. However, we recommend pushing for yet another round. Remember that the task is to empty the box of all the easy and obvious ideas. This is an energy-draining step, which is why we usually end the session with this step, taking up pattern-breaking thinking after an overnight rest.

# Manager's Checklist for Chapter 7

☑ Come to the meeting ready for brainstorming by posting the selected problem statement as well as a drawing of the ladder of abstraction.

☑ Strongly point out the importance of the ladder of abstraction to help create specific and actionable ideas.

☑ Participants brainstorm silently on 3" x 3" Post-it® notes and then share their ideas and build on them.

☑ Understand the importance of having participants silently write their ideas before sharing them. This ensures that groupthink does not limit the range of possibilities.

☑ At all costs, avoid the temptation to have the facilitator capture all the ideas on a flip chart with discussion, for the reasons presented in Chapter 3.

# Thinking Out of the Box: Breaking Patterns

W hy should you want to think out of the box? The simple answer is that it gives you unexpected solutions to your problems that are always more innovative than solutions that result from "standard" brainstorming.

Recall that you can easily get new and useful ideas just by "standard" thinking (brainstorming), but in today's competitive environment that's not nearly good enough. What you need is a way of creating unexpected ideas that are so new and so innovative that no one has yet conceived of them.

We all think in patterns. As noted in Chapter 3, these patterns serve us well by helping us live our lives more efficiently, but they also keep us thinking within the box. So, to think outside the box, we must learn to break our thinking patterns. For this reason, we call the tools we use *pattern-breaking* tools.

## Experience the Power of Pattern-Breaking Thinking

Let's assume that you are the owner of a failing taxi service and you've created some ideas to improve your profitability, using the usual thinking processes. Undoubtedly you would come up with some of the following ideas:

■ Reduce costs by finding cheaper fuel, making the taxi routes more efficient, etc.

**SMART MANAGING**

### LEARN FROM EINSTEIN

Albert Einstein noted, "No problem can be solved from the same level of consciousness that created it." We could adapt that wisdom to our situation: "Better solutions come when we go above and beyond our normal thinking."

Why was Einstein such a great thinker? "It's not that I'm so smart," he explained. "It's just that I stay with problems longer."

Einstein also said, "Logic will get you from A to B. Imagination will take you everywhere."

- Clean up the taxis, and make them more attractive.
- Make sure the drivers know the local area and provide good service.
- Give the taxis a distinctive look.
- Station the taxis at prime locations during peak times.

All of these are good ideas that are new and useful, but none is particularly innovative, because they came through standard brainstorming. Any competitor can come up with any of these ideas very quickly.

So you ask me to help you come up with ideas. Once we have extracted all the ideas by just "normal thinking," we are in a position to break out of the box. One of the walls of our box is our set of assumptions that control how we think and limit us to usual ideas that anybody could have.

In the taxi business, some of the most basic assumptions we make without ever bothering to question are as follows:

**TRICKS OF THE TRADE**

### SHIFT INTO REVERSE

One of the easiest and most popular techniques for breaking through the walls of our box is to reverse the assumptions that we make as we think about the problem.

First, we list our most basic assumptions. Then we reverse each one, simply saying that it's not true. Our list of assumptions makes visible one of the walls of our box; reversing them punches through the wall, letting us escape from the box. Then we ask how we can use the concept of the reversed assumption to help us solve our problem.

- The driver drives the taxi.
- The passenger pays the bill at the end of the trip with cash.
- The passenger is the one who pays the bill.
- The passenger knows where he or she wants to go.

Reversing each of these assumptions leads us to the following:

■ The driver does not drive the taxi.

■ The passenger does not pay the bill at the end of the trip with cash.

■ The passenger is not the one who pays the bill.

■ The passenger does not know where he or she wants to go.

Now we take each reversed statement one at a time and we generate new ideas to solve the problem.

For example, what might we do to improve profitability if the driver isn't the one driving the taxi? What if the passenger drove the taxi?. How might that work?

A number of options suggest themselves: you might create a short-term rental whereby the customer drives the car only for a limited amount of time as needed. That was a breakthrough idea several years ago, since at that time rental car companies never rented for less than one day.

In fact, this idea has now been implemented in major cities such as Washington, DC, Boston, New York, Chicago, Atlanta, and San Francisco: cars are available at subway stops and other locations if you have arranged it in advance through the Internet, *www. Zipcar.com*. Customers pay for the length of time they have the car, and they leave it at pre-determined locations.

Another option is to create a "Fantasy Drive," with vehicles that many people would want to drive but could never buy, such as a Rolls-Royce, a Bentley, an 18-wheeler truck, an Army tank, and the like.

What might we do if the passenger did not pay at the end of the trip with cash? Then we would accept only credit cards or checks, reducing the chance of robbery.

## IDEAS HAVE SHELF LIFE

Breakthrough ideas, like the short-term taxi rental idea, always come with a shelf life that is sometimes all too short. Much like commercially packaged food, your ideas will grow stale and worthless over time if you do not act upon them. The short-term car rental idea proved to be such a winner that it has attracted competition, even from several of the big-name companies.

If your breakthrough idea is a winner, then you must act on it to scale up and commercialize before its shelf life is exceeded. Low sense of urgency is death to innovation. The first to market takes the market.

Suppose the passenger is not the one paying the bill. You might consider creating volume discounts for companies that need a lot of taxi service and having the companies prepay for a given number of trips per month. You might structure an arrangement with the local government to provide transportation for those on public assistance who need it.

What could you do if the passenger does not know where he or she wants to go? How about offering a tour service? You could provide specially painted taxis and knowledgeable drivers who could act as guides to the local attractions.

In this short example, our purpose is not to solve this taxi problem, but rather to illustrate how reversing assumptions can create new channels of thought that somehow eluded us when we were just thinking how to reduce our cost. We cannot say that you would never have come up with these ideas on your own, but we are sure that it would have taken a great deal longer, and most people would give up before coming up with these ideas.

### BREAK THINKING PATTERNS

When we participate in business brainstorming meetings, we're trying to create new ideas yet we find ourselves thinking down the familiar well-worn path of thought. If we think the way we've always thought, we get the same thoughts we've always had. How can we avoid this problem?

What we need is a way to break away from this well-worn path, so that we can see new opportunities. The techniques of pattern-breaking thinking do just that. They shake up our thinking and create new channels that we had not yet considered.

## Requirements for Pattern-Breaking Thinking

As team leader, when you wish to engage your team in pattern-breaking thinking, you will want to ensure that you do the following:

- Present a compelling challenge.
- Create an environment of playfulness and humor.
- Ensure diversity of participants.
- Provide an appropriate setting.
- Appoint people to capture ideas.
- Apply the tools of pattern-breaking thinking.

## Present a Compelling Challenge

Although I can illustrate the power of pattern breaking with a made-up problem, you will reap business benefit only when there is a *compelling challenge or problem that requires innovative ideas.* We discussed how to construct challenge statements in Chapter 5. Without a compelling challenge, people will find the exercise interesting and fun, but not very useful.

## Create an Environment of Playfulness and Humor

Using pattern-breaking tools requires that we think in a different way, making strange connections and sometimes sounding a bit silly. In an organization where it's not OK to have fun and where we only think about work in the most serious terms, this is going to be quite difficult, if not impossible.

As team leader, you can help set a climate of playfulness and humor by dressing very casually, using such things as puzzles placed on tables prior to the meeting, or perhaps asking participants to tell a funny or an embarrassing story about themselves. You will want to create a climate where participants feel safe in proposing unconventional ideas. The objective is to make it OK to think of weird combinations and unusual ideas that can serve as the springboard on which useful ideas are created. If you're serious about the outcome, you should be lighthearted about the process.

## Ensure Diversity of Participants

You will get a better result if there is a great diversity among participants. Diversity in problem-solving styles (see Chapter 12) is highly desirable. In addition, you might strive for diversity in age, academic background, and cultural background.

## Provide an Appropriate Setting

You will want to select a room that is not crowded, with plenty of room on the walls for flip-chart paper, preferably off-site so that distractions of the workplace are minimized. It isn't necessary to spend a lot of money taking your team off to a resort location. You just need a comfortable and relaxed surrounding with an effective process with effective pattern-breaking tools and a talented facilitator.

**Problem-Solving Styles** "Consistent individual differences in the ways people prefer to plan and carry out generating and focusing, in order to gain clarity, produce ideas, or prepare for

**KEY TERM**   action when solving problems or managing change"

That definition comes from *VIEW: An Assessment of Problem Solving Style*, by Edwin C. Selby, Donald J. Treffinger, and Scott G. Isaksen (Center for Creative Learning, 2002). Treffinger, the author of several books on creativity and co-author of *Creative Problem Solving* and *Toolbox for Creative Problem Solving*, makes an important point. "Instead of asking, 'How creative is this person?,' we have learned to ask, 'How is this person creative? What are his or her strengths? How do people channel and direct their creative and inventive energies?'"

You don't need to be an expert on problem-solving styles. Just try to gather people who think in different ways. In most work environments, differences in thinking stand out.

## Appoint People to Capture Ideas

Recall that in brainstorming with sticky notes participants wrote down their ideas silently and then discussed them. With lots of experience, I have found that, in pattern-breaking thinking, people must be free to think and not be required to write. For some reason, the switch from thinking to writing stops everything.

Participants who are good at creating ideas do not want to stop creating to start writing, and they usually will not do it. And then, if they should write their ideas, they have a difficult time getting back into the ideation mode. Therefore, in pattern-breaking thinking, you should identify one or two people to be responsible for capturing ideas while the others are free to create. The facilitator's job is to point out when the idea-capturing people need to write down the ideas, making sure they are captured accurately. The function of capturing ideas is extremely valuable for the group, so you should thank those participants who are appointed to serve as scribes. The scribes may create ideas as well, of course.

In addition, you may want to use sticky notes of a color different from that used in brainstorming, so that during idea selection you can tell by the color which techniques produced the most innovative ideas.

## Apply the Tools of Pattern-Breaking Thinking

The model for pattern-breaking thinking is shown in Figure 8-1. Our thinking is depicted as the dot inside of the double-walled box.

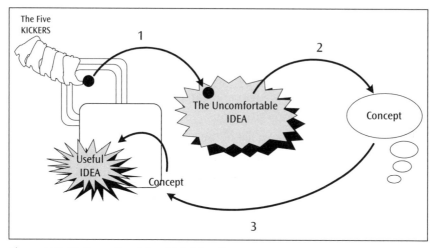

**Figure 8-1.** Pattern-Breaking Thinking Process

Now that we have emptied the box of easy ideas, the time has come to apply one of the kicker tools of pattern-breaking thinking to mentally boot us out of the box. This will cause us to mentally land somewhere outside the box. The ideas that arise at that point will usually be uncomfortable or so wild we would never want to do them.

Next, you will need to help your participants develop a more abstract idea (sometimes referred to as the *basic concept*) based on where you landed. This is a tricky step, but it gets easier with practice. (See the sidebar for an example.) Once you have the concept, then you ask the participants to create specific and actionable ideas for using that concept to solve the problem. This should be a facilitated discussion in which ideas flow freely from person to person. The facilitator's task is to know when a specific and actionable idea has surfaced so the scribes can capture it.

# Creative Thinking Tools

Five creative thinking tools (kickers) are presented here:

1. Reverse hidden assumptions.
2. Force associations.

3. Make comparisons.
4. Take other perspectives.
5. Start from an outrageous idea.

As I describe these tools, I will use our case study for examples.

## Reversing Hidden Assumptions

One of the walls of our "box" is composed of the assumptions that we make about the problem we are working on. We constantly make assumptions about what we can and can't do, what will and what won't work as we think about any situation.

With this tool, we make a list of the assumptions we make about the issue that are so commonplace and basic we never bother to question them; that's why we call these the *hidden* assumptions. Next, we simply reverse each assumption, saying that it is not valid or true. We select those reversed assumptions that are interesting or humorous or outrageous and we ask how the reversed assumption could be used to solve our problem. Here are some of the assumptions that were made about the computer company in the case study.

1. Computers are packed in shipping boxes. (Computers are not packed in shipping boxes.)
2. The customer pays for the computer. (The customer does not pay for the computer.)
3. We are open during normal business hours. (We are not open during normal business hours.)
4. We don't take trade-ins. (We accept trade-ins.)
5. The salesperson takes an order from the customer. (The salesperson does not take the order from the customer.)
6. We have a display area in the store. (We don't have a display area in the store.)
7. Customers need service. (Customers don't need service.)
8. We display products only, not our services. (We display our products and explain our services.)
9. Our service person is our employee. (Our service person is not our employee.)

The participants decided that the reversed assumptions 2, 3, 4, 6, 8, and 9 were interesting. Using these as a springboard, the following specific and actionable ideas were created:

1. If the customer doesn't pay, we could sell computers in bulk to local employers, who would then sell them to their employees at zero interest.
2. Students could rent computers for use in our store, and the rental would apply to purchase.
3. Stay open 24 hours for college students.
4. Give traded-in machines to schools or charities and earn a tax deduction.
5. Display our service by showing an open computer or parts and how to install them.
6. Contract our service to computer science or engineering students.

---

### PUBLICIZING A PRICE POLICY

A major retailer wanted to remain number one in home appliance sales in the United States against price competition from big-box retailers. The retailer used reversing hidden assumptions to help create an innovative idea that has been extremely effective.

A market research study had revealed that several million potential customers shopped the retailer's appliance sections every year but left to search for better prices and then purchased from competitors. Participants in the workshop listed perhaps 25 hidden assumptions about these lost potential customers.

The most interesting was "These people know what we have to offer." That assumption was reversed as "These people do not know what we have to offer." That led the participants to make a long list of things that the retailer offers.

One that stood out was its price-match policy. The participants decided to create an in-store campaign to educate potential customers about this benefit. They created the "Tear-Away" program: the sales associate fills out a three-part form with a potential customer; in large prominent letters at the bottom is the message, "We Will Match Any Price."

In its first year, the program increased revenues by several hundred million dollars. Was it easy? No, it required two full days. Was it worth it? Yes!

---

## Forcing Associations

Sometimes called *free association*, this tool works by forcing an association between the problem situation and something completely unrelated, usually determined by chance. Sources can be magazine pictures, things seen on a walk through the mall, items drawn from a bag, or words pulled randomly from a book.

Following the process diagram in Figure 8-1, the next step is to list the concepts surrounding that item or word and apply those concepts to developing solutions to the problem. In the case study, the word "dehumidifier" was taken at random from a dictionary. The following concepts emerged:

1. Change of state: gas (water vapor) to liquid (water)
2. Accumulates water
3. Make the invisible visible
4. Drawing in a resource
5. Improves comfort

Of those concepts, the most attractive appeared to be #3, making the invisible visible. In thinking about how to get closer to the customer (the problem statement), inspired by that concept, the following ideas were quickly generated:

- Make the customers more visible to us with an up-to-date database.
- Get a customer to write a testimonial for an advertisement saying how helpful the computer store has been.
- Make it a habit to ask every customer about any problems.
- Have customers post tips and techniques to our bulletin board for all to see.
- Summarize customer letters of support into a brochure.

## Making Comparisons—Metaphoric Thinking

In metaphoric thinking, we select a system we understand well and make comparisons between that system and the system of our problem situation. This comparison is usually done on a flip chart. In the left column, list the components of the metaphoric system, and in the right column, list the corresponding components of the problem situation.

Here's an example from our case study.

Selected metaphoric system: a garden. Our situation: a failing business.

SERPENTINE SILLINESS SLIDES INTO SUCCESS

A beverage company wanted to sell more of its product to its biggest single target market, 21- to 35-year-old single males. Brainstorming yielded nothing new. The facilitator decided to force associations. He asked a participant to pull something at random from a bag containing a variety of items. It was a rubber snake. Participants listed the following concepts:

1. Some snakes are nocturnal. Concept: sponsor evening events.
2. Some snakes prepare their prey for eating by injecting the animals with digestive enzymes. Concept: prepare the target market for what's to come—build excitement.
3. Snakes shed their skin to grow. Concept: get a fresh start.

The concept of a fresh start was particularly interesting to this group. From that concept the members quickly developed the innovative idea of holding a contest and offering the winners, as a prize option, a fresh start in life. The fresh start could mean paying off credit cards or car loans and providing tuition for further education.

| Garden | Failing Business |
|---|---|
| sun, soil, water | raw materials |
| plants | production machinery |
| gardener | business director |
| pests | overly demanding customers |
| harvest | profits |
| weeds | competitors |
| scarecrow | ? |

In metaphoric thinking, we must find some component of the metaphoric system that has no counterpart in our problem situation. In our example, the scarecrow in the metaphor of the garden has no counterpart in our problem situation. The next step is to ask about the concept of the missing component (in this case the scarecrow) and then apply that concept to create ideas to solve the problem.

## Taking Other Perspectives

This tool works by selecting someone or a group that is very well known *and* highly provocative and then asking what that person or group might do to solve the problem. Some examples of well-known and provocative people or groups have been Al Capone, Gandhi, a rock musician, the

> ### SCARECROW TACTICS
>
> **FOR EXAMPLE**
>
> This tool was used to help a fiberglass insulation manufacturer deal with a difficult but major customer. The customer was purchasing a huge percentage of the fiberglass plant's output and was dictating production scheduling, delivery, price, and terms. When thinking about the concept of the scarecrow, the workshop participants realized it was "a false representation of danger to a pest." They saw this demanding customer as the pest and began to think what they could do to create a representation of danger that would convince the customer that it was in its interest to become more of an ally and less of an adversary. Quickly someone suggested forward-integrating into the customer's business, to compete in that market, which the manufacturer actually threatened to do, and the difficult customer became much less demanding.

Pope, a rapper, and a lawyer. The better known and the more provocative, the better. This tool works because the person or group selected would certainly approach the problem differently than most people. The following are the concepts that came from the case study, where the provocative perspective was that of a rock musician.

**Concepts from Rock Musician**

- Creates large following of loyal fans
- Makes provocative music videos
- Writes own songs
- Very loud
- Good at self-promotion
- Appeals to the young but disliked by the old

In the case study, the following ideas for getting closer to the customers were created based on the concepts from a rock musician:

- **Concept: Loyal fans.** Specific idea: Create a partnership program with the largest customer groups, tailored to meet their needs.
- **Concept: Makes videos.** Specific idea: Sponsor an amateur video featuring the youngest and the oldest customers. Put it on YouTube, and play it in the store.
- **Concept: Writes own songs.** Specific idea: Sponsor contest for customers to write advertising jingles; make the best jingle part of the amateur video.

- **Concept: Self-promotion.** Specific idea: Have local entertainers perform at the store, targeting younger groups during the day and older groups in the evening.
- **Concept: Appeals to the young.** Specific idea: Involve younger customers to develop a store image and merchandising plan.

## Starting from an Outrageous Idea

This tool works by simply asking, "What is so outrageous we would never ever consider doing it because it is so shocking, illegal, or disgusting?" If an idea meets this criterion, by definition it will be outside of your box as well as outside of everyone else's box. Then we list the concepts behind the outrageous idea and ask how we can use the concepts to create innovative solutions to the problem.

In the case study, these outrageous ideas were suggested:

**Outrageous Ideas for Getting Closer to the Customers**

- Make sales presentations in the nude.
- Throw cold water on all the customers entering the store.

It is clear that you would never do either of these outrageous ideas. And that's what makes this tool work, because it leads you to think in ways you never would have considered.

Some concepts that arise from those two outrageous ideas are listed below:

- If you're in the nude, there is nothing to hide.
- If you throw cold water on every customer, they will be surprised and shocked and surely will complain.

Some of the specific actionable ideas that flow from these concepts are as follows:

- Make sure sales people know everything about the product. Explain the good and the bad points of each system and software up front. Transparency and openness always build trust, which can translate into customer loyalty.
- Make it easy for customers to complain by giving each a complaint form and asking him or her to fill it out. The results can alert to weaknesses of which you were unaware or that you did not consider important enough to remedy. Taking complaints seriously can increase

customer loyalty. You might also reward the complainer with "complaint points" that can be redeemed for merchandise or training.

## Idea Pool

Now that all the ideas have been generated through brainstorming and through pattern-breaking thinking, we need to put them into the *idea pool*. The idea pool is a number of flip-chart pages taped to the wall, onto which the sticky note ideas are affixed. Figure 8-2 shows the idea pool from the case study after the ideas have been grouped according to subject matter.

The idea pool is the starting point for convergence, an implementation step that will be described in Chapter 9.

## Manager's Checklist for Chapter 8

☑ Pattern-breaking thinking allows you to mentally get "out of the box" to find more innovative ideas.

☑ You must empty the box of the usual ideas through brainstorming before using pattern-breaking tools.

☑ Our most basic or hidden assumptions about the problem situation form one of the walls of our mental box, keeping our thinking inside.

☑ The team leader must set a relaxed and playful climate so that pattern-breaking tools can be effective.

☑ The facilitator can make pattern breaking easier and more effective through practice.

## Customer Knowledge ③

- Make the customers more visible to us with a database.
- Maintain detailed customer list with every purchased component so when someone calls, we know what they have and when they got it.
- Make regular use of opportunities to communicate with customers to make it easy to stay close.
- Send customers a birthday card printed in a color on a DC system to advertise our color printers and to say happy birthday.
- Know who customers' children are and what ages.
- Send letters asking if a child needs a computer when time to go to school.

## Easy Complaint Process ⑤

- Get more complaint tickets the more you complain—makes it fun to complain.
- Call back within 30 days to check for problems.
- Make it easy to air problems but inside a private room that is quiet to avoid distractions.
- Assign every customer his/her own personal contact person at DC, including home phone number.
- Make it fun for a customer to call you about a problem.
- Complaint tickets for merchandise.
- Phone customers after the sale to check satisfaction.
- Have DC employees ask customers what problems or questions they have that they have never been asked.

## Go to the Customer ⑥

- Drive the computers to the customer for a trial.
- Require every DC employee to visit one major customer each week.
- We have displays in the local mall on Saturdays covered by volunteers.
- Go to trade shows in the area.
- Open 24 hours for college students.
- Tour the university and high schools to show products and services.
- Go to the customers on Monday and Tuesday on a one-on-one basis.
- Create a tour of business applications in the community.
- We go to people's homes or places of business, offer price quotes, and see where they would place the computers.
- Go to the grade school level and other classes for the children of PC owners.
- Establish branch office near main business district.

## Customer Give-Away ⑨

- Give one free maintenance call per year.
- Give free mouse pads with logo.
- Give free power bars with computer purchase.
- Give free games with the purchase of a PC.
- Give free diagnostic disks to customers.
- Give customers templates for software applications.
- $10 gift certificate for each new purchase of $100 or more of merchandise.
- Games night for adults to purchase software for kids.
- Refund the additional warranty dollars if customers do not use us for the warranty.
- Appreciation night for all past customers with 10% off all merchandise.
- Have drawing after Christmas where one whole system gets paid off, or people get dollars back if already paid.
- Allow 30-day return on software.
- Allow companies to buy in bulk from us and sell to employees at no interest.
- Apply additional warranty coverage to the first time repair.

## Used Computer Market ④

- Open another branch store selling only rebuilt computers.
- Students rent computers to use in our store—rent applied to purchase.
- Give old business machines to university students.
- Take machines back for recycle to encourage owner upgrade and support the community.

**Figure 8-2.** Case study idea pool

# Convergence and Implementation

It's a great mistake to neglect the convergence stage of problem solving. Many people believe they can just pick the best ideas and move on. You will get the best results when you thoughtfully apply agreed-on criteria within a structured process for idea selection.

## Staged Criteria Process

This process is orderly and structured, which makes it effective and relatively fast. It works because we use only one criterion at a time, avoiding the complication of mixing the criteria up as idea selections are made. Here are the criteria that we use, in the order of use:

1. The idea would be highly effective in solving the problem.
2. We currently have the capability to implement the idea. (*Capability* means that we have the knowledge and/or technology or we can easily obtain or create what we need. It specifically does *not* mean that we have the *resources*.)
3. The idea is likely to gain broad organizational support and is a fit for our strategic direction.

Please note that we have *not* included anything about resources. We've found that good leaders almost always want to include resources as a criterion. We know this is a serious mistake at this point, because once the idea has been developed further, if it's good enough, resources can be reallocated from existing programs.

# Convergence Process

At this point the idea pool is large and contains ideas from brainstorming written on yellow sticky note paper and ideas from pattern-breaking thinking written on blue paper (or any color other than yellow).

**Step 1.** Count the yellow notes, count the blue notes, and enter those two totals in your version of the flip-chart table shown in Figure 9-1 (which contains numbers as an example), in the Idea Pool row under Yellow Ideas and Blue Ideas. Add the two totals, and put the sum under Total Ideas.

If the problem has been worked on before, the idea statistics chart (Figure 9-1) will usually show more selected ideas from pattern-breaking thinking than from brainstorming. This shows the value of going beyond brainstorming to create innovative ideas to old problems. If, however, the problem is new and has not been considered before, then you're likely to find most of the selected ideas coming from brainstorming, because these are the "low-hanging fruit," ideas that are easier to implement and must be tried first. We will come back to this table later, in step 5.

| | Yellow Ideas* | % of Total | Blue Ideas* | % of Total | Total Ideas |
|---|---|---|---|---|---|
| Idea Pool | 350 | 70% | 150 | 30% | 500 |
| Idea Grid | 24 | 33% | 48 | 66% | 72 |
| Final Selection | 2 | 40% | 3 | 60% | 5 |

*Yellow ideas (yellow notes) are from brainstorming.
*Blue ideas (blue notes) are from pattern-breaking thinking.

**Figure 9-1.** Idea statistics (example)

**Step 2.** Calculate each participant's prorated share of 15 percent of the total number of ideas. For example, if there are 500 ideas and 12 participants, then 75 (15 percent of 500 ideas) would be divided by 12. The share per participant would be 6.25, which we round down to six ideas each.

**Step 3.** Ask that each participant step to the idea pool and select the prorated share of ideas (six in our example), based only on criterion #1 above, *The idea would be highly effective in solving the problem.* Tell the participants to disregard the color of the sticky notes as they make their selections. Participants should physically remove the sticky notes from the idea pool and hold onto them for the next step.

**Step 4.** Apply criterion #2, *We currently have the capability to implement the idea.* To do this, construct the idea grid, a large version of Figure 9-2, on flip-chart paper taped to the wall.

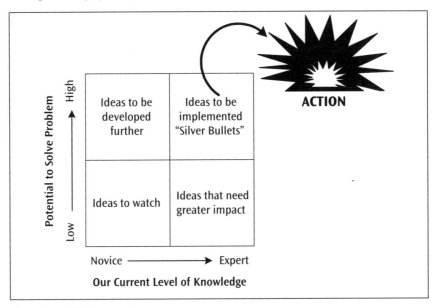

**Figure 9-2.** The idea grid

One by one, ask participants to step to the idea grid, read their selected ideas, and suggest the quadrant where each idea should be put. Encourage discussion among participants about current capability and potential, so that the ideas are positioned properly on the idea grid. If there are duplicate ideas, they should be put together and treated as one.

Note that the vertical axis is for the potential to solve the problem. The top 15 percent of the ideas have already been selected based on potential to solve the problem, so most of the sticky notes will probably be put in the upper half of the idea grid.

As an example, Figure 9-3 shows results from the case study.

**Step 5.** Count the number of yellow and blue notes on the idea grid, and place the numbers into your version of Figure 9-1.

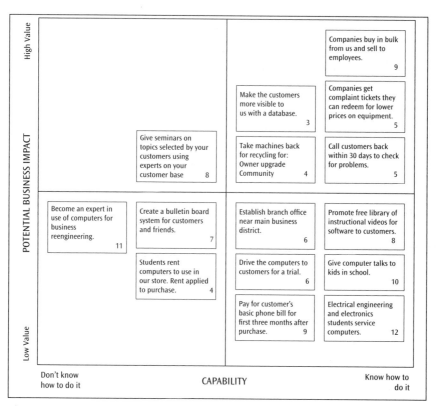

**Figure 9-3.** Idea grid from the case study

**Step 6.** Select three to five great ideas from the idea grid that are worthy of implementation. Many times those ideas will be found in the upper right quadrant, labeled "Silver Bullets." These ideas have high potential for solving the problem and are easily implemented, so it's expected that the three to five ideas will be selected from that quadrant. Criterion #3, *The idea is likely to gain broad organizational support and is a fit for our strategic direction,* should be used here. We use one of two ways to select the best ideas from the idea grid. The first way is to have the participants vote. The second way is to have the sponsor or client make the selection, since he or she almost always must agree with the final selection anyway.

In the case study, the idea that was selected for implementation was "Companies buy [computers] in bulk from us and sell [them] to [their] employees." This idea will be used to illustrate the rest of the process of planning for implementation.

**SMART MANAGING**

## Be Pragmatic

In my experience, the best method of selecting the winning ideas from the idea grid is to simply ask the sponsor to do the final selection while the participants are on a short break, explaining the reasoning behind their selections. The sponsor often knows things that others do not and is in the very best position to make such decisions. Should the participants do the selecting, the sponsor must agree on the ideas to be implemented anyway, no matter how the vote turns out. Having the sponsor make the final selection is a pragmatic approach that saves time, anguish, and perhaps some disagreement.

# Opportunity for Personal Commitment

Once the ideas have been selected from the idea pool, 85 percent of the original ideas will remain unselected. An important "side step" is to give participants the opportunity to select any previously unselected idea that strongly appeals to them—so long as they commit to taking the next step to decide if the idea merits full scale-up.

You will want to create a flip chart labeled "Personal Commitments" and have participants place these ideas on the flip chart with their names on them. This becomes one of the items to audit during the implementation process. The sidebar describes the result of one such event.

**FOR EXAMPLE**

## The Power of Personal Commitment

We were engaged by a minerals and pigments company in the Northeast to help develop new product ideas. One of the ideas that was not selected was small reflective flakes to give a deep iridescence to automobile paint. Two of the participants expressed great personal interest and together selected it as their Personal Commitment. They worked on it on their own as a separate line of work in their laboratories. They even worked on some weekends. Their work was successful and yielded a pigment for transparent paint that gives a beautiful deep sheen that did not exist before.

This example shows the importance of allowing people who have a deep passion for an idea the opportunity to work on it. Venture capitalists say that you should invest in the person, not the idea. This is an example of the truth of that statement.

# Idea Implementation

Now that the top ideas have been selected, the time has come to put together the beginning of an implementation plan. The next steps are intended as only a start. You will have to give a great deal more attention to them after the workshop is over, starting by including the right people for each of the ideas selected.

You will want to have two or three participants work together on each of the selected ideas. Working together, they should complete the five worksheets in the Appendix. The specific ideas chosen and the implementation steps planned from the case study will be shown in the rest of this chapter as a model for you when using the worksheets in the Appendix.

## Strengthen the Idea

Before beginning an implementation plan, we need to strengthen the selected ideas. Using Worksheet #1 in the Appendix, list the benefits of implementing the idea. These might be the arguments you would use to sell the idea throughout the organization.

In the case study, the benefits of implementing the idea could be

- higher sales;
- a good route to getting closer to the customer;
- saturating the local market to reduce PC-MAX threating;
- follow-on sales from employees for software, etc.

With every new idea, there are concerns and potential problems, which we address by completing Worksheet #2 in the Appendix. List the concerns, and develop at least one action to overcome each concern. This is like contingency planning, so if things go wrong we have a backup plan.

Figure 9-4 shows the case study list of concerns and actions to take for the idea that companies would buy computers in bulk from us and sell them to their employees.

On Worksheet #3, list the critical steps that must be taken early to establish viability of the idea. Ask yourself, "What are the critical hurdles the idea must overcome in order for it to be viable?" These are the tests that need to be run early, so that if there's a significant barrier, we'll find it early and at low cost.

| CONCERNS | ACTIONS TO TAKE |
|----------|-----------------|
| Additional salespeople needed to support higher sales. | Establish sales quota of 10X the salary of the new salespeople. |
| Local business doesn't want to favor any one supplier. | Make a strong business case in favor of sole source. |
| Companies find a lower-cost supplier and cancel contract after six months. | Establish a rebate program that pays only at the end of 12-month contract. |
| Relatives of our company and local businesses may give the appearance of impropriety. | Prevent company relatives from working with local business relatives in any sales negotiation. |

**Figure 9-4.** Case study concerns and actions

In the case study, the following critical tests were uncovered:

1. Develop typical hardware and software packages, and estimate potential profit margin.
2. Develop package software deals on programs needed by most companies.
3. Create typical proposal for company management, and test for viability.

### Ensure Diversity of Participants

As mentioned in Chapter 8, you will get better results with greater diversity among participants, in the convergence stages of thinking as well as in the divergent stages. In addition to diversity in age, education and training, cultural background, experience, and work responsibilities, diversity in problem-solving styles is crucial.

Different styles bring different values and perspectives and ways of approaching problems, ideas, and solutions. This is important when generating ideas and when testing possible solution.

## Start Planning the Project

Worksheet #4 shows the tree diagram that is step 1 in project planning. Write your selected idea in the leftmost box and then the critical steps in the middle, followed by detailed actions that must be taken for each of the critical steps.

Figure 9-5 shows the case study idea, "Companies buy [computers] in bulk from us and sell [them] to [their] employees," in the leftmost box, the major steps to make it happen, and the detailed actions for each major step.

This chart is filled out from left to right, but it is checked for accuracy and completeness by going from right to left. So, with Figure 9-5, start at the right and ask, "When each of the details for the first major component step has been accomplished, will that be sufficient to have accomplished that step?" If the answer is yes, then move on to the details for the next major component step. However, if the answer is no, then you must consider another detailed action that might be needed to accomplish that major component step.

> ### USE "CHICKEN TESTS"
> The story is told of a jet engine manufacturer that invested millions developing carbon-fiber-reinforced turbine blades. One of the tests that jet engines must pass is to ingest a bird in flight without catastrophic failure. The standard test involves tossing a chicken from the supermarket into the intake as the engine is running. When this was done, the chicken destroyed the engine, causing great financial difficulty for the company because the test was done late in the development cycle. Decide what the "chicken tests" are for your project, and run them early, while there's time and resources to recover.

## Develop a Project Timeline

Using Worksheet #5, develop the beginnings of a project timeline for the implementation of your idea. Place the specific actions from Worksheet #4 in the left column. Place individuals' names or functions in the boxes with reference to when actions should begin and end in the implementation process.

Although this is nothing new to project managers, it may be helpful as you begin to think about who needs to do what by when to bring your idea to fruition. In most workshops the right people to do the project timeline are those who will be responsible for making it happen. Almost never are they all in the workshop. As team leader, you will want to engage them fully to help craft a project timeline that is reasonable and

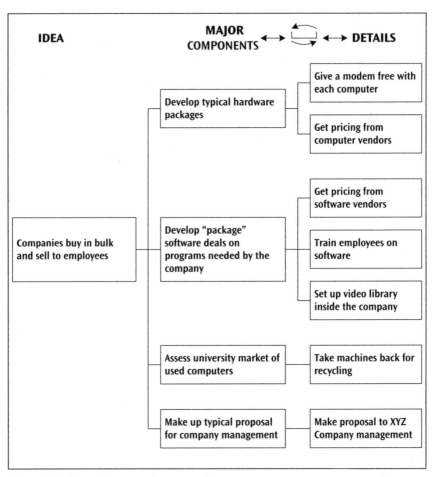

**Figure 9-5.** Tree diagram of case study

auditable. As you audit from month to month, you will want to make adjustments as needed to reflect delays or accelerations in the program elements.

## Manager's Checklist for Chapter 9

☑ Allocate sufficient time to the convergence and implementation steps of innovative problem solving so that you gain full value from it.

☑ Be sure to apply the idea selection criteria one at a time in the staged criteria process.

☑ Confirm with your team members that the criteria recommended for idea selection are the right ones for your situation. If they are not, change them by consensus.

☑ Make full use of the worksheets in the Appendix. These can form the basis for auditing implementation progress.

☑ Be sure to set up a mutually agreed-on schedule for auditing progress with your team. Then follow through. What gets measured gets done.

# Setting the Climate
# for Innovation

The working climate that the leaders create is the single biggest factor governing the success of the organization's total innovation effort. We consistently see that this is so, and many other experts in the field make the same strong assertion.

## The Essence of the Right Climate

Many organizations reorganize the company or remodel the workplace, providing new furniture and equipment, hoping for innovation to happen. Some companies even set aside and equip a room for creativity.

While a certain level of comfort is certainly necessary to avoid distractions that interfere with work, paying attention only to the superficial, physical aspects of the workplace misses the mark badly. What really matters is establishing a climate for innovation—a direct result of the policies and practices with respect to people and work that are set by leaders at every level of the organization.

The most beautiful settings can be hell if the people

> **PUTTING THE "NO" IN INNOVATION**
>
> FOR EXAMPLE In one case, a *Fortune* 100 company created a "creativity room" with beanbag chairs, brightly painted walls, and plenty of white boards to capture ideas. However, it was kept locked and any potential user had to justify the need in order to get the key. That company is now out of business.

> ## CLIMATE FOR BUSINESS PERFORMANCE
> **SMART MANAGING**
>
> "The climate—how people feel about working at a company—can account for 20 to 30 percent of business performance." That's the assessment by Daniel Goleman, Richard Boyatzis, and Annie McKee, in their book, *Primal Leadership* (Harvard Business School Press, 2002).
>
> They cite research results to back up that assessment. "In a study of nineteen insurance companies, the climate created by the CEOs among their direct reports predicted the business performance of the entire organization: In 75 percent of the cases, climate alone accurately sorted companies into high versus low profits and growth."

are assigned jobs that are wrong for them (see Chapter 12), are treated poorly, are denied resources, or believe that their ideas are not really wanted or valued. As Allan Fahden, author of *Innovation on Demand,* puts it, "Hell is still hell, no matter how many times they remodel."

Conversely, a workplace with a merely adequate setting can be wonderful if people are assigned jobs that are right for them and the leaders set the right climate for innovation.

If an atmosphere of mistrust, fear of failure, and enforced conformity prevails, employees will not be innovative, even if the organization provides innovation training and leaders exhort employees to "Be more innovative."

## An Exercise: Creativity at Work

Think about a time when you were creative at work. It could be a time when you solved some critical problem, created something new, improved a process, or developed a particularly innovative insight about an issue. In the space

> ## NOT "ALL WORK AND NO PLAY"
> **SMART MANAGING**
>
> During his time as CEO of Southwest, Herb Kelleher focused on the people aspects of work, creating a climate for innovation that made Southwest employees well known for taking themselves lightly but their jobs seriously. Flight attendants often sing their announcements to the tune of popular songs and on takeoff have even let the peanut packages slide down the aisle! All this creates a fun and festive atmosphere—and year after year Southwest is listed among the top five Most Admired Corporations in the U.S. in *Fortune* magazine's annual poll.

**DON'T CRUSH CREATIVITY** Alan G. Robinson and Sam Stern, in their book, *Corporate Creativity* (Berrett-Koehler Publishers, 1998), note that 50 percent of the world's engineers live and work in Russia, but not nearly 50 percent of the innovations come from Russia, primarily because of the poor environment for innovation. Why? They quote a Russian engineer: "A bad system will beat a good man every time."

below, write a brief account.

_____

_____

_____

_____

_____

Now list some of the things that your leader did to help you be creative. What did he or she do to create a supportive work climate?

_____

_____

_____

When a number of people did this short exercise, we found a huge coincidence of things their leaders had done to facilitate innovation. As it turns out, these repeat items generally fall within the 10 dimensions of the innovative climate that are described below. The qualities that make for a great place to work are the same qualities that foster innovation. The working climate is far more important than any of the superficial niceties of a windowed office, amenities like a health club or a running track or free soft drinks and snacks, or the newness or the appearance of the office and its furnishings.

Dr. David Braun, former distinguished 3M Company Fellow, confirms that 3M leaders pay much more attention to the working climate set by the leaders than they do to the physical surroundings.

Richard Florida, in *The Flight of the Creative Class* (HarperCollins, Publishers, 2005), points out that graduating students usually move to centers of *talent, technology,* and *tolerance,* as opposed to choosing to live in areas that are low in the "three T's." That means building civic centers, sports stadiums, and new shopping malls in low three-T areas does little to cause high-talent people to want to live there. To us this sounds strikingly similar to the situation of talented people who want to work in organizations that have created a supportive climate of innovation, people for whom that climate is far more important than all the physical trappings.

## Intrinsic Motivation and Extrinsic Motivation

Another parallel of the importance of climate over physical trappings is found in the importance of *intrinsic* motivation over *extrinsic* motivation.

## Hygienic Factors and Motivating Factors

Frederick Herzberg, in his early work on employee motivation in the 1950s and 1960s, discovered that the things that create satisfaction and motivation on the job are different in kind from the things that create dissatisfaction ("One More Time: How Do You Motivate Employees?" *Harvard Business Review*, September/October 1987, Vol. 65, No. 5). Herzberg identified a set of *hygienic factors* and a separate set of *motivating factors* that work together to cre-

**Extrinsic Motivation** A stimulus that causes people to try to achieve some goal based on the prospect of **KEY TERMS** gaining a reward. Extrinsic motivation works well when the task is simple and clear and it follows a prescribed method, or when the task is to increase a quantity, such as exceeding sales quotas.

**Intrinsic Motivation** A stimulus within people that causes them to act simply for the pleasure of the activity itself. Intrinsic motivation comes from an internal desire that doesn't depend on the prospect of a reward.

**MAKES SURE THE MOTIVATION IS RIGHT** Study after study has shown that creativity and innovation flourish with intrinsic motivation and dies when rewards are offered up front (Alfie Kohn, *Punished by Rewards* [Houghton Mifflin, 1993]). We should keep this point in mind as we think about the motivation of team members for creativity and innovation.

ate job satisfaction (see sidebar). Hygienic factors remove limiting negatives, while motivating factors provide psychological growth. Once an organization has provided the hygienic factors, the stage is set to provide the motivating factors.

What is intriguing is that Herzberg found that the opposite of job dissatisfaction is not job satisfaction, but rather *not dissatisfaction*. And con-

## Herzberg's Hygienic and Motivating Factors

| Hygienic Factors: | Motivating Factors: |
|---|---|
| Pay and benefits | Achievement |
| Job security | Recognition |
| Status | Work itself |
| Company policy and | Responsibility |
| administration | Advancement |
| Relationships with coworkers | Growth |
| Physical environment | |
| Supervision | |

sequently the opposite of job satisfaction is not job dissatisfaction, but rather *not satisfaction.*

I diagram the dissatisfied-satisfied continuum in Figure 10-1. In the middle is what I call the "NOT" state—a point of being neither dissatisfied nor satisfied. The important thing about Herzberg's work is that the absence of hygienic factors creates job dissatisfaction but their presence does not create job satisfaction. Similarly, his motivating factors create job satisfaction, but their absence does not create job dissatisfaction.

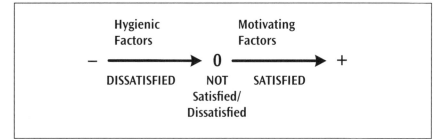

**Figure 10-1.** The "not" state of job satisfaction

Once the hygienic factors have been provided and you are now in the "NOT" position of Figure 10-1, understand that adding more hygienic factors will not create job satisfaction. It's like being extremely thirsty and desperately needing water. However, once you've enough water, more won't make a difference. To use a workplace example, just providing more salary without a sense of accomplishment or recognition won't result in

**FIRST HYGIENIC, THEN MOTIVATING**

SMART
MANAGING

The astute manager needs to understand what causes job dissatisfaction and what causes job satisfaction and that one is not the
opposite of the other. The manager's main job is to remove the
negatives by providing adequate hygienic factors and to provide
motivating factors.

One caution: providing the motivating factors without first removing the
negatives by providing hygienic factors will backfire and result in cynicism
among your people. For example, imagine the response you would get for
applauding employees for an outstanding job on a difficult task (providing
recognition) but at the same time promoting your poorest supervisor, whom
everyone intensely dislikes (rewarding poor supervision). In my opinion, you
must first provide hygienic factors, removing the negatives that cause dissatisfaction, and then make sure the motivating factors are in place.

job satisfaction. Dr. Tom L., a research engineer in an industrial R&D laboratory in Virginia, quit his job because, in his words, "All they know how
to do is give me more money."

So what does all this have to do with innovation? Innovation cannot
flourish in a climate of job dissatisfaction. People will do the minimum to
keep their jobs. For innovation to flourish, people need to be motivated
to do a good job, to go beyond what most leaders would know how to get
from their employees. They must be intrinsically motivated.

# Power of Intrinsic Motivation

Curious people do things that interest them simply for the enjoyment of
doing them. These kinds of activities are intrinsically motivated. People
who are motivated intrinsically will find ways to improve their work,
solve a critical problem, or create a whole new initiative, all on their own,
and only because they were personally interested.

It's this kind of motivation that you want your team members to feel
as you foster creativity and innovation. To reinforce their intrinsic motivation, you need to welcome their efforts and enthusiasm when they excit-
edly show you their developments. You can quickly kill enthusiasm and
intrinsic motivation with early critical judgment pointing out what's
wrong. By far the worst de-motivator would be for the leader to criticize
and discount an idea from a team member and then present it to others as

his or her own, without attribution. I personally know a high-talent professional who left his company because of such greedy management behavior. (By the way, when people leave, it's usually because of their supervisors, not because of the company.) On the other hand, there is no limit to accomplishment when a leader works hard to give away all the credit.

Extrinsically motivated people do things in order to gain a reward of some sort. Offering pay for ideas is an example of attempting to motivate people extrinsically when, in fact, creativity must be motivated intrinsically. You will get what you pay for, but it's probably not what you want. A number of large companies have had the experience of promising to pay for ideas and just motivating a few employees to submit a huge quantity of ideas of no conceivable value. Those employees were gaming the system to add value to their paychecks but not to the company.

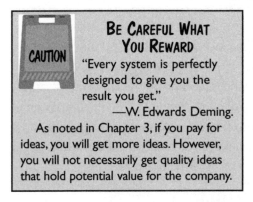

**BE CAREFUL WHAT YOU REWARD**

"Every system is perfectly designed to give you the result you get."
—W. Edwards Deming.
As noted in Chapter 3, if you pay for ideas, you will get more ideas. However, you will not necessarily get quality ideas that hold potential value for the company.

Extrinsic motivation works well when the job is mundane or routine and all you want is more work or faster work. However, for creativity and innovation, intrinsic motivation is what is needed.

In very interesting parallel work, Edward Deci (University of Rochester) and Mark Lepper (Stanford University) have found we can convert intrinsic motivation to extrinsic motivation simply by paying for it. Children who love to play sports for the sheer joy of it are intrinsically motivated. Is it any wonder why highly paid professional sports figures sometimes go on strike if they feel like they're not paid enough? The motivation for their behavior, originally intrinsic, has been converted into extrinsic by large rewards, and the behavior will stop if the rewards are perceived to be too low.

Now, no one is going to refuse an extra amount of money as a reward for a job well done, and extra payments are certainly justified on occasion. The key is to not pay so much that it's considered a bribe for future

> ### PAY FOR PLAY ENDS THE GAME
> An apocryphal story about pickup baseball games among neighborhood children makes this same point. The kids made a lot of noise playing on the empty lot, which bothered the man who lived next to the field—who understood this *intrinsic-extrinsic swap*. One evening he asked if he might pay them each $1 to let him watch the game. Of course they excitedly agreed. The next evening he offered them 50 cents each, and again they agreed. A third evening he offered 25 cents, and they accepted grudgingly. The fourth evening he offered nothing—so they marched off the field and refused to play because they were not getting paid. He got the silence he was looking for.

performance, so that the reward itself becomes the next goal. The prospect of a reward causes people to find the quickest route to winning it and the reward becomes the focus of their efforts.

> ### READING FOR PIZZA
> A story from Peter Scholtes about a friend's daughter ("Reward and Incentive Programs Are Ineffective—Even Harmful") illustrates this point as well.
> "Emily had been a good student, an avid reader ... that is until Pizza Hut got into the reward business. It seems Pizza Hut provided teachers with coupons for free pizzas to be awarded to a student when he or she had completed a book. [Emily] started reading shorter and less challenging books or just skimmed longer books, so she could get more coupons. Meanwhile, Emily's classmates also started reading more books. Even those who were not readers started reading. The books they read were short and simple, but at least these kids were reading something. The students who, like Emily, were avid readers, switched their reading preference to short, simple books. Eventually, however, Pizza Hut's reading-for-pizzas campaign ended; and so did the reading—all reading—by those who used to be avid readers of challenging books as well as by those who didn't read. . . . With pizza coupons no longer available, the kids in the class felt that there was no longer a reason to read."

Nobel Prize winners never undertake a line of work in order to win the prize. Anyway, the prize is usually awarded many years after the work has been done. And no Nobel Prize winner continues to do work because he or she wants another Nobel Prize. The winners do the work for its own sake: they are motivated intrinsically.

# Dimensions of the Climate for Innovation

Let us examine the dimensions of the climate for innovation. I will present real stories of real people showing how leaders set the climate for innovation that paid off handsomely. As you read these stories, think how you might apply some of their principles within your own team.

A supportive climate for innovation is one in which creativity and change are encouraged. Based on the pioneering work of Göran Ekvall in Sweden some 50 years ago, it is now possible to quantify the climate for innovation. Ekvall's work has been further refined and validated by Scott Isaksen and others, who have clarified nine dimensions of the climate for innovation, dimensions that can be measured using an instrument called the Situational Outlook Questionnaire (*www.soqonline.net*, info@cpsb.com). We've added a tenth dimension, "Value for diversity of problem-solving style," described in Chapter 12.

1. Challenge and involvement
2. Trust and openness
3. Freedom
4. Risk taking
5. Idea time
6. Idea support
7. Debates on the issues
8. Interpersonal conflict (negatively correlated)
9. Playfulness and humor
10. Value for diversity of problem-solving style

In our work we have found the most important of these 10 dimensions of the climate are items 1–6. Sadly, items 1–6 also tend to be the dimensions most often in the greatest need of improvement in the organizations we have evaluated. I will now discuss each one in some detail.

## Dimension 1: Challenge and Involvement

This is the degree to which people are challenged by their work and the degree to which they are emotionally involved in their work and committed to it. If the jobs are challenging and the employees are highly involved in problem solving, this will facilitate intrinsic motivation. This will lead people to create and innovate simply because they are interested in the subject.

In that situation, innovation flourishes. In addition, the climate is dynamic, electric, and inspiring, and people find joy and meaning in their work. In the opposite situation, people are disengaged, and there are feelings of alienation and indifference. Employees commonly feel apathetic and they lack interest in their work. You can hardly expect this kind of atmosphere to breed innovation.

As a foundation for producing greater innovative output, people in the organization must personally feel a compelling challenge. The nature of this compelling challenge can be at the extreme of personal or business survival or a burning internal drive to accomplish some task or achieve some worthy goal. For example, in the movie, *Apollo 13*, because their survival depended on it, the crew developed some very innovative approaches to solving the problem of scrubbing lethal carbon dioxide gas from the air in the space capsule. Other compelling challenges can be the opportunity to improve lives through education, to rid the world of a specific deadly disease, or to ensure the safety of air travelers. The compelling challenge could be as simple as providing exceptional service to your customers, as do Nordstrom, American Express, and the Ritz-Carlton hotels.

**DON'T NEGLECT ANY EMPLOYEE WITH A HEAD**

Here is an hourly worker's comment on the annual HR employee satisfaction survey at a DuPont synthetic fibers plant: "For 20 years you have paid for my hands and you could have had my head for free, but you never asked." This is a perfect example of how to exclude people and not involve them in their own work.

How do you fix this problem? Institute an effective system to ask for and use ideas from everyone. (See Chapter 8.)

Whatever form it might take, one of the team leader's most significant responsibilities is to communicate a clear and compelling challenge that the team members will want to adopt as their own. This is what creates the need for innovative thinking and action.

## Dimensions 2, 3, and 4: Trust and Openness, Freedom, and Risk Taking

These three dimensions of the climate are so tightly intertwined that it is difficult to discuss one without crossing into the other. Clearly, trust and openness form the foundation on which freedom and risk taking are built—and without freedom and risk taking there can be no innovation.

> **FOR EXAMPLE**
>
> ### CRITICAL IMPORTANCE OF TRUST AND OPENNESS
>
> Lou Holtz, the famous football coach, in one of his videos ("Do Right," *www.atsmedia.com*), explains that players always silently ask the following three questions of their coach:
> 1. Can I trust you?
> 2. Are you committed to excellence?
> 3. Do you care about me?
>
> We strongly believe that every member on your team silently asks the same three questions of you. If they conclude that they cannot trust you, the answers to the other two questions don't really matter.

It is generally accepted that trust occurs when people are known through past experience to be competent, reliable, and sincere. However, when it comes to innovation, trust needs to be more than just the product of competence and reliability. Trust that leads people to admit mistakes early so they can be corrected or to ask for help requires a level of openness that also results in greater personal vulnerability.

This is called *vulnerability-based trust* and was beautifully described by Patrick Lencioni in his book, *The Five Dysfunctions of a Team* (Jossey-Bass, 2002). Team members must learn to acknowledge their weaknesses, their mistakes, and their need for help, and they must recognize the strengths of others. Openness and vulnerability are inseparable, two sides of the same psychological coin.

Trust and openness are both variables, and each is the cause and the effect of the other at the same time. In the language of systems thinking, they form a reinforcing loop (see Figure 10-2), because when one increases, the other does as well, creating a virtuous spiral upward. However, if one of these two variables is decreasing, the other will follow right behind, creating a vicious spiral downward.

**IMPORTANCE OF OPENNESS AND TRANSPARENCY**            SMART

Think about a leader you mistrust so much that you might even hide bad information from him or her. Now think about the opposite kind of leader, someone with whom you would share most any information because you trust him or her so much. The            MANAGING biggest difference between these two people is more than likely the level of openness and transparency they showed toward you from the start. The leader you trust the least probably shared the least with you, and the leader you trust the most was more transparent and open with you. Which type of leader do you wish to be?

One of the modern business themes is transparency in leadership, because it is so critical to business success (*Transparency* by Warren Bennis, Daniel Goleman, and James O'Toole [Jossey-Bass, 2008]). Transparency builds the kind of trust that allows people to reveal and then correct small mistakes before they become big ones.

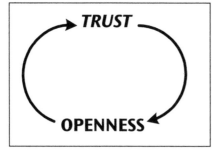

**Figure 10-2.** The reinforcing nature of openness and trust

Openness always comes first. As a team leader, you will want to find ways to be as transparent as possible with your team members, sharing as much information as possible and admitting your own mistakes to them.

I decided to share the monthly cost sheets with my R&D group in a research laboratory. Up to that time, engineers had no idea of the real cost to keep them on the payroll. It turned out to be a huge amount of money, many times their salaries, because of overhead and benefits that they'd never considered in the costs of compensation. This made them very conscious of how they spent time and money. One team member even published the cost of our team meetings! It made us all aware of the need to be good stewards of our resources.

Nothing builds trust as much as transparency and honesty and handling mistakes in a positive way. Figure 10-3 (developed with Cal Wick, the founder and CEO of Fort Hill Company, which specializes in Follow-Through Management™) shows the cause-and-effect relationships that are involved, for better or for worse, when mistakes are made.

**SMART**

**MANAGING**

## SHOW THAT YOU CARE ABOUT PEOPLE

Robert Levering says in *A Great Place to Work: What Makes Some Employers So Good (and Most So Bad)* (Random House, 1988), "The constant replenishing of trust reservoirs is the single most distinguishing characteristic of great workplaces. Employees recognize that the company cares about them and respects them."

In *The Wisdom of Teams* (Harvard Business School Press, 1993), Jon R. Katzenbach and Douglas K. Smith show that a high-performing team is one whose members all take personal responsibility for the growth and well-being of the others. This kind of atmosphere builds trust among team members and demonstrates mutual care.

This is a systems thinking treatment of this issue. It shows us that leaders need to do two things when expectations aren't fully met. First, they fix learning instead of blame, so that the next attempt will have a better chance of success. Second, they build vulnerability-based trust by admitting their own mistakes and engaging their team in the learning. This sets the example for team members to share their concerns and mistakes as projects are carried out and results don't fully meet expectations.

Others have noted, and we concur emphatically, the importance of exposing small mistakes early so they can be corrected at low cost in order to avoid making the biggest mistake of all—missing the target. If the

**FOR EXAMPLE**

## TRUST, OPENNESS, AND FREEDOM GET RESULTS

In 1999 DuPont was commercializing a new film product used for food packaging. This business unit was using PACE (Product and Cycle Time Excellence), a phased process to speed up product development. At an interim review, one of the teams had to report that a technical failure threatened to derail the entire project unless a suitable solution was quickly found.

Instead of blaming the team members for uncovering the problem so late in the process, the leaders thanked them for bringing it to their attention so promptly; commended them for finding the problem before the product was commercialized; and asked how long it would take to find a solution. The team said it needed three months. The leaders allowed them that extra time and told them that they were confident that such a highly skilled team would come up with a path forward. The team members were so energized by that response they developed a workable solution in a month. This is an excellent example of a climate of trust, openness, and freedom.

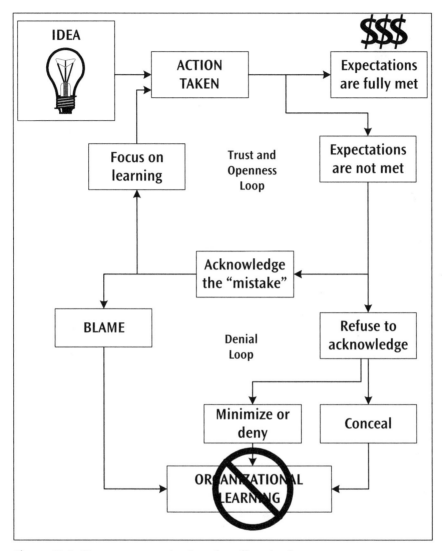

**Figure 10-3.** Two ways organizations handle mistakes

people associated with mistakes get punished, you will find few people willing to try new things or admit mistakes.

But what about accountability? Are we asking that you not hold people accountable for their decisions and actions?

*No!* It is more a question of what you hold people accountable for. We suggest that you hold people accountable for the learning that can be gained when a mistake is made.

**Mistake** Usually an error resulting from inadequate attention, insufficient or faulty knowledge, poor reasoning, and/or bad judgment.

Unfortunately, we don't have a word that means "a well-reasoned attempt that didn't meet expectations," so for this type of partial failure I'm using the word "mistake."

Figure 10-3 shows that someone takes action to implement an idea. Sometimes, in ideal situations, expectations are fully met. However, most often expectations are not fully met; we are calling that failure to meet expectations a "mistake." The level of trust that the person has with his or her team leader will help that person to decide whether to admit the "mistake" so that it can be corrected or to conceal it.

If it is concealed, there is no organizational learning. Concealing a mistake is equivalent to stealing intellectual property, since the organization paid for learning but is being denied its value. (Most companies will immediately discharge anyone found guilty of stealing company property. You might make the case that stealing intellectual property by concealing mistakes is grounds for dismissal.)

If, however, the person decides to admit the "mistake," then the team leader must decide whether to fix learning or to fix blame and punishment. If blame and punishment are the focus, then the learning will be for everyone to conceal mistakes in the future. If learning is the focus. the

### CLIMATE OF FEAR CAUSES COMPANY TO FAIL

**FOR EXAMPLE** The owner of an aerospace company in Maryland was very punitive and unforgiving when mistakes were made, and everyone knew it. The company was making very precise metal cylinders for military rockets. One machinist had mistakenly turned a precision cylinder to a thinner wall thickness than specified. Instead of admitting his mistake, he created a second cylinder, which, when slipped over the first and welded to it, looked perfect. It met the measurement specifications and was sold.

Unfortunately, the rocket exploded, and the failure was traced to the defective cylinder. The punitive owner ultimately lost his business because of this mistake, which could have been acknowledged, discussed, and fixed. Make sure that everyone knows you are tolerant of mistakes and that you focus on the learning, so that you prevent the biggest mistake of all—missing the target.

whole organization becomes smarter, and the next attempts are more likely to work. This can form the foundation of a learning organization. Leaders should lead by example—and what better way to model the behavior you want than to be the first to admit to your own mistakes to your team and engage them in a discussion of what went wrong, so that everyone learns.

David Tanner, former director of the DuPont Center for Creativity and Innovation, reports in his book, *Total Creativity in Business and Industry* (Advanced Practical Thinking, Inc., 1997), that a company president created the "Golden Egg Award" to emphasize the importance of learning rather than blaming:

> The sharing of mistakes and other misadventures was a favorite part of monthly meetings of a group of presidents of Ann Arbor MI businesses. The enthusiasm members felt for these sharings led to the idea of a "Golden Egg Award." As one member put it, "I want to hear it from the member who got egg on his face trying out his idea." A trophy was soon put together with the help of a L'eggs® pantyhose container shaped like an egg and some gold spray paint. Presentation of this award for the best "mistake" of the month became a standard part of their meeting, and the trophy itself added an important new dimension. The winning president was expected to take the trophy back to his office and leave it on his desk for the entire month. The presence of the Golden Egg raised questions from visitors, and led to telling the questioner how he got the award. It also gave the president the chance to be a model for treating mistakes as opportunities to learn how to do it better rather than as a situation requiring blame. It legitimized the importance of learning from our failures and successes.

During idea implementation, serious resources are consumed. People want to feel safe in allocating resources, not afraid of personal negative consequences if the idea doesn't fully meet expectations. In short, it must be OK to not fully meet expectations when trying new ideas.

## Dimension 5: Idea Time

To what degree do people have time to think things through before having to act? That's important in a climate for innovation. People need time to think.

**CAUTION**

## Don't Assume That a "Mistake" Is a Failure

In the 1980s the U.S. Navy, in conjunction with the U.S. Coast Guard, commissioned Battelle Memorial Institute to find a new, more effective anti-fouling bottom paint for ships, a paint that would prevent barnacles and other hard species from attaching to the boat beneath the water line.

The goal was a totally clean boat surface. The primary focus was on a paint to slowly release toxic chemicals as its mechanism of action. One of the approaches was ruled a "mistake" and totally unusable, since it grew an ugly living slime. This approach was abandoned by the sponsors and the Navy.

However, Dennis Guritza, a biological scientist who was one of the reviewers, noticed that, in addition to the slime, there were no barnacles or any other hard marine species attached to the panels. He ultimately found that the slime mimicked the slime on fish skin, and barnacles don't grow on fish.

Today the disruptive technology that grew the unsightly slime is being commercialized in a breakthrough nontoxic anti-fouling coating that is environmentally friendly and will last for many years (*www.luritek.com*). It has also, because of its low-friction surface, resulted in increased boat speeds and reduced fuel consumption. It promises to revolutionize boating and shipping, aquaculture, and commercial water-handling industries with its nontoxic and long-lasting properties as a true platform technology in biomimicry. The original mistake was to assume that a squeaky clean "no life" surface was superior to a "managed life consortium" like the slime that is proving to be a superior solution in many unexpected ways.

Picture this: you are making progress on your new product development assignment when a major customer calls your unit head with an urgent problem and you find yourself on the next flight out to fix the problem. The pressure for fixing problems steals time from innovation. The result is "innovation burnout."

So, how can we create idea time? You might want to make idea-friendly spaces, such as the office coffee station and perhaps the cafeteria or eating area. You might consider installing whiteboards with magic markers. You might write on each whiteboard an important problem to be solved and invite comments; keep it updated, and respond to the comments. If your team members must account for their time so that projects can be charged, you might create an "idea time" account and ask the members to use it appropriately. If time is being charged to such an account, you might ask to see a result every now and then.

---

### THE POWER OF TRUST

From the 3M Company, known for its culture of innovation, comes a story of the technology that made microwave popcorn possible, told by one of the inventors, Curt Larson.

"My story is about the trust that my Research Manager and Technical Director had in me when I was doing completely new microwavable food packaging invention and development. I was given freedom to lead with my ideas, energy, knowledge, and desire to work with customers to create something new. After many experiments to find a material and system for making microwave popcorn pop to a much higher volume, we identified microwave-active materials as a bag component that were then in their embryonic stages of development.

My two cohorts (from sales and marketing) and I returned from a development trip with a potential customer with our first order, for 1.2 million microwave susceptor patches, even though we still had only made them in the lab. The customer had given the order to us because he had seen our determination and initial success. We marched into my manager's office to declare the good news. He looked at us with big surprise and his broad smile and said, 'I didn't believe that you could do it, but thank you!' I remember replying, 'But you never told us that you didn't believe—you just encouraged us!' My manager and director . . . trusted that my enthusiasm would pay off if they did not get in my way. What a fun climate to work in! And, wow! It sure did make me conscientious to produce results!'"

---

## Dimension 6: Idea Support

No management behavior is more powerful than providing support for new ideas—and no management behavior does more damage than withholding support. You can think of stories in your own experience that confirm the essential truth of this statement.

Here's yet another example of creating an innovative climate by providing idea support. It happened in a chemical research laboratory in which one of the technicians, Phil Harman, was an avid bass fisherman. He regularly competed in bass fishing tournaments, the object of which is to catch the most weight of fish in the shortest time. Being an inventive type, he replaced the dull, lifeless, rubber thread that hides the hook on bass fishing lures (called the "skirt") with brightly colored but transparent Lycra thread that he had made in the laboratory. To his amazement, his modified lures worked like a charm, and many of his closest fishing buddies got the same result, catching more fish than normal.

---

**IDEA TIME**

**FOR EXAMPLE**

An excellent example of the importance of *idea time* comes from Ted Jagusztyn, who worked for many years as an engineer at the Carrier Corporation. He said he had to leave in order to be innovative because there was no thinking time.

When he retired, he began to think, "How can we use the heat discarded by the air-conditioning systems in our buildings to replace the additional energy we use to create hot water?" Strongly believing that he needed to look at the big picture from the customer's perspective in order to gain real insight, he spent three years with hotel owners in Mexico, who told him about their energy needs. As a result, Ted created and is now commercializing his CoTherm equipment for hotels. It takes the sun's heat, normally discarded by the air-conditioning system, concentrates it through a compressor, and yields essentially free hot water for the entire hotel. He has demonstrated savings upwards of $10,000 per month per hotel. Not only does the hotel save money, but the environment also wins because the carbon footprint is greatly reduced (*www.cotherma.com*).

As you set the climate for innovation in your team, think how you might create idea time. You will want to foster a climate of innovation so that your innovators keep innovating for your team—and don't go elsewhere.

---

He went to his manager and asked for a few dollars to build a skirt-making machine. His manager rebuffed him with the words, "We don't have a fishing lure program in this laboratory." Because he believed in his work, Phil then went to another research manager known to be more supportive, who authorized the few dollars he needed for the next steps. Phil worked with a machine shop to build a machine that allowed him to make skirts in large quantities for market testing. This idea ultimately turned into a commercial product for DuPont (LumaFlex® Lures), and U.S. Patent No. 5,007,193 was granted with Phil as an inventor. The brightly colored elastomeric fibers also found use in Koosh® Balls.

When Phil retired, he received a handsome check as a token of thanks for his work. In Phil's words, "You cannot stop if someone tells you, 'No.' Keep searching until you find a 'Yes.' The support I got from that manager was what I needed to keep pushing. Without it my invention would have died quickly."

David Tanner tells this story that shows the power of a capable and impassioned team with 100 percent consistent and strong support from

**$UPPORT INNOVATIVE IDEAS**

SMART

The DuPont Co.'s $EED program was conceived as a way to provide funds for employees who had ideas they wanted to try that their business units could not fund. The grant application form is shown in Figure 10-4, courtesy of DuPont. Every application was reviewed by a group of volunteer senior professionals who decided on funding. The expenditures funded could include travel and equipment and supplies, but not pay. The recipient of an award was required to account for funds at the end of the project and could request more if needed or return any unused funds.

MANAGING

During the 10-year history of the program, DuPont invested some $2.9 million in $EED ideas and realized over $20 million in additional revenue as a result. The greatest value, however, was not so much the revenue but rather the climate for innovation that was promoted by removing organizational barriers to trying new ideas.

In your budgeting process, you might want to consider adding a line item titled "Unplanned Activities" and make this amount available for new things that surface during the year. We can never be wise enough on January 1 to know all the great new ideas worthy of a try that will arise during the year.

top leaders to rapidly bring an idea to market. DuPont knew that customers wanted carpets that resisted soil and stain better, but no company had effectively dealt with the staining problem. Research chemist Armand Zinnato discovered technology in a "bootleg effort" that dramatically improved stain resistance, a discovery that ultimately resulted in DuPont Stainmaster® carpet. However, taking his invention to market would be a major challenge, because it would require a significant change in the process for making the fiber and in the way the carpet mills turned that fiber into carpet.

The research director realized its potential and committed himself and his R&D organization to full implementation. The management steering team had representatives from marketing, manufacturing, R&D, product management, and tech marketing. Their fundamental charter was to do whatever it took to beat the competition to the marketplace, since it was known that competitors were hot on the trail with similar leads. In the end, this need meant merging the demonstration and scale-up phases into one continuous effort in order to meet the target launch date.

**$EED GRANT APPLICATION**

**$EED**
Dollars to Encourage Entrepreneurial Developments

Return to: $EED, Experimental Station, Bldg. 326/Room 315

Name: ______ Department: ______

Job Title: ______ Address: ______ Telephone: ______

Current program assignment/SBU: ______

Title of idea: ______ Amount requested: ______

Explanation of market need and your idea: ______

How does your idea fit with DuPont's strengths and interests? ______

Milestones to be accomplished with this grant, including timing and resources needed to accomplish them (include, if possible, a summary of how you would allocate $EED funds): ______

Have you considered patent protection for your idea? ______

What other resources (funding or in-kind contributions) would be available to you from your SBU or elsewhere in DuPont? ______

DUPONT

**For $EED Comittee Use Only**

Grant # ______ Amount ______

Contact ______ Date ______

Signature: ______

Date: ______

(Please attach additional information or sketches, if necessary, to support your business plan)

**Figure 10-4.** DuPont's $EED Grant application

The team members met regularly to coordinate the multiple tasks, such as fully defining the technology, organizing the carpet mill certification program, and implementing new manufacturing processes in DuPont's plants. In addition they had to structure a consumer advertising campaign and the retail marketplace interface. The steering team quickly expanded its scope to establish working relationships with other DuPont divisions and with the advertising firm BBDO, which created the award-winning TV commercials used to kick off the market introduction.

The powerful vision of what the product could do in the marketplace was a unifying and electrifying force that kept the team focused. And the strong capabilities of the people working on the project enabled the team to drive forward without a lot of backtracking and stopping to check in. The technical leader of the carpet mill program was given free rein to do whatever he saw necessary to deal with key issues, even exclusive use of a company jet so he could quickly go wherever he was needed.

All of the pieces of the program fell into place at the right time. DuPont announced Stainmaster®—and two competitors quickly followed with announcements of their stain-resistant carpets. But the high level of Stainmaster® performance, its well-planned market launch, and its extensive and superbly executed advertising strategy took the U.S. carpet industry by storm.

**MANAGERS MAKE INNOVATION WORK** **SMART**

**MANAGING**

The willingness of DuPont's senior managers to assign people from all key areas to the Stainmaster® team, to give them a clear challenge with the necessary resources, and to empower them to act was central to DuPont's ability to beat its competitors in the marketplace.

## Dimension 7: Debates on the Issues

This dimension is the degree of positive tension—people actively disagreeing with each other about the issues, but not about each other.

Like it or not, many team members are likely to agree with you simply because you're the team leader. When that happens, there can be no productive debate in which people objectively disagree about the issues. If you are the kind of leader who is truly open to new ideas and to changing your mind, read on. If you're not, then skip the remainder of this section.

If your team members do not already know your position on a subject, you might want to delay telling them until you have heard all the debates. If they already know your position, you can still spark debate by taking an opposing view and asking what might happen if the team adopted that approach. As team leader, you will want to avoid the fatal mistake of asking for team input and debate when your mind is already

## PROVIDE GUIDANCE, NOT SOLUTIONS

Experienced professional executive coaches often think they know the solutions to issues posed by their clients. However, the really great coaches ask questions that get their clients to examine a number of alternatives, rather than immediately offering their own solutions. In most cases, clients are able to develop their own solutions that are better than solutions proposed by the coaches. Also, when the clients come up with solutions, they're more likely to follow through as well.

made up, the team members know your feelings, and you know that you aren't going to change your position no matter what they say. It's far better to be transparent and simply say, "This is my decision," and give a few reasons that make sense.

## Dimension 8: Interpersonal Conflict

To what degree do people engage in conflicts? This is the only one of the 10 dimensions that is negatively correlated with the climate for innovation. Conflicts differ from debates in that they result from tension between and among personalities rather than ideas. Interpersonal conflicts are always destructive in any team, because they waste energy and distract from working on the problems. Sometimes team members take sides, further widening the dispute and further hampering productivity.

Team leaders must eliminate this negative energy drain, even if it means relocation or termination. If a conflict arises, it could be an excellent opportunity to review the social contract and demand that each of the warring parties answer the question, "What don't you understand about your commitments?" If the fighting continues, you may have to

**TOOLS**

## SOCIAL CONTRACT

A social contract (discussed in Chapter 11) is an agreement between management and a team that states what management will provide and what the team will provide, with key deadlines. This contract establishes expectations for all parties and documents their commitment.

make a tough decision about further employment for one or both of the warring parties. You cannot afford to allow one or two rotten apples to spoil the barrel.

DuPont Surlyn® resins are used in over 90 percent of the outer coverings of golf balls manufactured today. A team working on improving Surlyn® resin technology experienced great turmoil and upset when the well-respected team leader retired from the company. The new leader was a young and very talented woman, but this change caused conflict within the team. Dr. Robin Karol, an internal consultant, helped the team diagnose its prob-

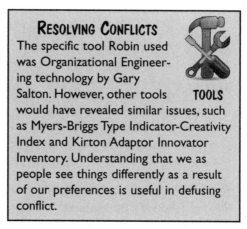

**Resolving Conflicts**
The specific tool Robin used was Organizational Engineering technology by Gary Salton. However, other tools **TOOLS** would have revealed similar issues, such as Myers-Briggs Type Indicator-Creativity Index and Kirton Adaptor Innovator Inventory. Understanding that we as people see things differently as a result of our preferences is useful in defusing conflict.

lems by helping the members understand each other better and how they needed to work together as a team. Robin used well-known tools (see sidebar).

Bringing the issues out into the open and discussing goals and motivations ended the interpersonal conflicts and helped the team to be productive again.

## Dimension 9: Playfulness and Humor

How relaxed is the workplace? Is it OK to have fun?

An informal and relaxed atmosphere where stories and laughter are heard characterizes a playful environment. Leaders need to bring lightness to the office. They may create an atmosphere of informality, probably through their dress and easy-going style, while being serious about doing the work and meeting objectives. In the opposite situation, there is little playfulness and humor, greater formality is required, and it's a "business only" approach. Creativity requires a playful approach, and great formality means low creativity.

In the movie, *Doubt*, the nuns are depicted in a joyless existence run by a very stern mother superior, whereas the priests enjoy relaxed fun and laughter headed by a playful monsignor. You probably have experienced workplaces with similar differences. Which kind of leader do you want to be?

---

**SMART**

## START WITH A FUNNY STORY

To set the stage for playfulness and humor in a brainstorming session, you might tell a funny story about yourself, and then ask others to do the same if they wish. I have done this for quite some time and am never disappointed because it instantly makes everyone a participant rather than just an observer, melting any "ice" away quickly.

Here's an example. At an insurance company in Hartford, Connecticut, Dan recalled the time in the fourth grade when his teacher invited the students to wear their Halloween costumes to school. He told his mom he wanted to dress as a cowboy, but she was more "out there" and convinced him to dress as a cowgirl and surprise everybody. He reluctantly agreed, and she purchased the costume. She dressed him in a pink hat, skirt, boots, and makeup and dropped him off at school and drove away. Unfortunately, for the "cowgirl," Dan was *a day early*! He was mortified—and he was reminded of it for years, until graduation allowed him to escape.

---

## Dimension 10: Value for Diversity of Problem-Solving Style

Valuing diversity in problem-solving style is critically important to innovation. Different styles bring different values and viewpoints, enriching problem-solving results. Valuing diversity means including people of diverse backgrounds, abilities, and interests in the business process, especially when they don't think like you do.

While it is a natural human tendency to hire and promote people "just like us," Robert Sutton, in *Weird Ideas That Work* (The Free Press, 2002), suggests that we hire people who make us uncomfortable. If the job candidate is competent and has the skills your firm needs, then Sutton suggests that negative emotional reactions are reasons you should hire the candidate.

Strive to make everyone, especially people known to think in unusual ways, feel valued, since you understand they have much to contribute because of their different thinking styles. It's really an issue of inclusion, making sure that no one is omitted or ostracized because of his or her preferred style of thinking and problem solving. In the opposite case, people who have "off-the-wall" ideas are often not taken seriously and tend not to be given much organizational authority. Pejorative descriptions may be used, such as "space cadet," "not serious," "loose cannon," or "troublemaker" (see Chapter 12).

As team leader, you will want to personally seek out the "different thinkers" and include them in your working meetings whenever possible. You might consider making a presentation to your team on thinking-style diversity and its importance to your business success.

## Implement Ideas

The first step in the process for innovation (simplified in Figure 2-2) is idea generation. This activity grinds to a halt when there is no time for ideas. This one dimension is usually the first to fall victim when organizational urgency matters more than importance. The pressure to do more with less squeezes us all, leaving little time for thinking about ideas. It takes energy to deliberately allocate time for ideas.

The final step of the process for innovation is idea implementation. That is where organizations most often fall short in the innovation process. If idea implementation stops, then ideas that have not been implemented pile up, causing "back pressure," which causes the idea generation process to stop also. In short, if you stop implementing ideas, then people will stop generating ideas.

Has your leader ever called your group together to brainstorm some ideas to solve a particular problem? Undoubtedly your answer is yes. Has it ever happened that none of these ideas was ever implemented? Again, you probably answered Yes. If the leader calls your group together again and asks for more ideas, there will be little energy or interest, because nothing happened last time and group members will have little faith that their effort will be worth the time.

The lesson: find ways to take action on ideas so that the idea generation process will remain vibrant and healthy. Keep your team informed on progress and decisions regarding their ideas.

## Manager's Checklist for Chapter 10

☑ Always remember that setting the proper climate for innovation is your most important job. Without a favorable climate, there won't be any innovation.

☑ Develop a working knowledge of intrinsic and extrinsic motivation.

☑ Memorize the top 6 of the 10 dimensions of a climate for innovation.

☑ Trust and openness is the most important dimension of the climate for innovation. Building trust through openness and transparency comes first, last, and always.

☑ Continually ask your team members what would help them be more innovative. Then, do your best to provide those things for them.

☑ Facilitate intrinsic motivation by eliminating the negatives associated with Herzberg's hygienic factors. Then, work to provide some of his motivating factors.

☑ Practice just saying yes more often than no.

☑ Memorize the five pitfalls (Chapter 2)—

- Working on the wrong problem
- Judging ideas too quickly
- Stopping with the first good idea
- Obeying rules that don't exist
- Failing to get sponsorship and build coalitions

—and work hard to avoid them.

☑ A quick way to kill creativity in your team is for you to speak first.

☑ Implement ideas or people will stop generating ideas.

# Leading Innovation in Teams

These are the tasks for leaders of innovation in teams:

1. Understand motivation, and set the climate for innovation (Chapter 10).
2. Develop a social contract with the team members.
3. Maximize the power of mission/vision.
4. Ensure alignment.
5. Lead change.
6. Create a self-sustaining culture of innovation.

## Develop a Social Contract to Set Expectations

Carol Kobza, formerly of Hallmark Cards Inc., identified methods for supporting new product development teams. One item of overriding importance was to develop a contract between management and each team, stating what management will provide and what the team will provide, with key deadlines. This is exactly the same point that Joseph Cangemi and Richard Miller make in "Breaking out-of-the-Box in Organizations" (*Journal of Management Development*, Vol. 26, No. 5, 2007, pp. 401-410). In their view the formulation and fulfillment of a social contract between the organization's leaders and the team is a necessary precondition to developing a healthy climate for innovation and creativity. This process sets expectations for all involved.

**Social Contract** An agreement between management and a team that **KEY TERM** states what management will provide and what the team will provide, with key deadlines. This contract establishes expectations for all parties and documents their commitment.

Cangemi and Miller points out that when new people come to work, they usually sign an employment contract spelling out the material aspects of work. However, the things that aren't spelled out can be more important than the material items; developing a social contract is a way of giving voice to the unspoken items. Cangemi also emphatically points out that the "right kind" of senior leader at the top is necessary for the social contract to work. The leader needs to have a strong sense of trust and be willing to listen and learn. He or she cannot have a dictatorial and micromanagement style. There must be a climate of openness and trust.

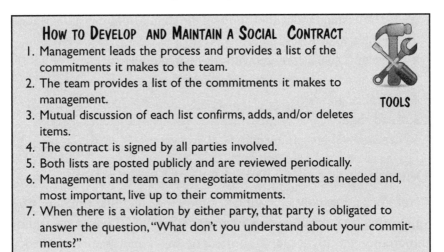

### How to Develop and Maintain a Social Contract

1. Management leads the process and provides a list of the commitments it makes to the team.
2. The team provides a list of the commitments it makes to management.
3. Mutual discussion of each list confirms, adds, and/or deletes items.
4. The contract is signed by all parties involved.
5. Both lists are posted publicly and are reviewed periodically.
6. Management and team can renegotiate commitments as needed and, most important, live up to their commitments.
7. When there is a violation by either party, that party is obligated to answer the question, "What don't you understand about your commitments?"

**TOOLS**

In a case study, the authors attribute to the climate for innovation created by the social contract innovations in processes brought about by team members at a Southern USA plant. There the operating costs were cut by 25 percent, productivity was improved by 15 percent, production increased by more than 50 percent, and inventories were reduced by 40 percent. The authors contend that these vast business improvements could not have happened without the very effective social contract

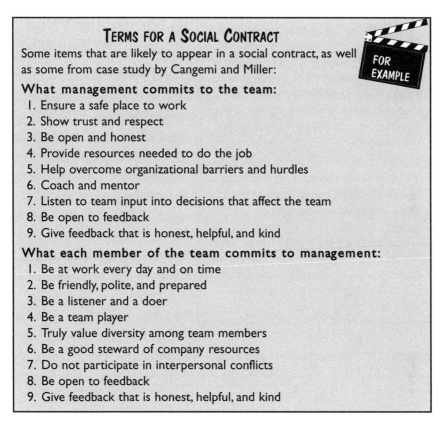

**Terms for a Social Contract**

Some items that are likely to appear in a social contract, as well as some from case study by Cangemi and Miller:

**What management commits to the team:**
1. Ensure a safe place to work
2. Show trust and respect
3. Be open and honest
4. Provide resources needed to do the job
5. Help overcome organizational barriers and hurdles
6. Coach and mentor
7. Listen to team input into decisions that affect the team
8. Be open to feedback
9. Give feedback that is honest, helpful, and kind

**What each member of the team commits to management:**
1. Be at work every day and on time
2. Be friendly, polite, and prepared
3. Be a listener and a doer
4. Be a team player
5. Truly value diversity among team members
6. Be a good steward of company resources
7. Do not participate in interpersonal conflicts
8. Be open to feedback
9. Give feedback that is honest, helpful, and kind

between management and employees. In short, it formed the foundation for a climate of innovation and employee involvement and commitment.

## Ensure Organizational Alignment

Innovation can be thought to fall into one of two categories, *incremental* or *radical*.

In thinking about resource allocation, you might find it helpful to look at the relationship between the type of innovation or technology and the type of markets on the matrix in Figure 11-1. This analysis is well known in the business world.

If you were to represent your existing projects as circles on the matrix, with the size of the circles representing the amount of resources assigned, you will have constructed a bubble chart that allows you to quickly see your current allocation of resources. With this information, you might decide to change resource allocation.

**KEY TERMS**

**Incremental Innovation** Innovation to improve existing systems, making them more competitive, better, faster, and/or cheaper. For an excellent example refer to Cangemi and Miller's case study described earlier in this chapter.

**Radical Innovation** Innovation to create totally new technologies, products, business models, and/or ways of thinking about customer needs that perhaps the customers have not even articulated yet. For an excellent example, refer to Chapter 10 and the breakthrough non-toxic anti-fouling boat-bottom paint that is a radical departure from traditional toxic anti-fouling paints.

# Maximize the Value of a Compelling Mission/Vision

The compelling challenge is most effectively expressed as a compelling mission or vision. Good leaders paint compelling missions or visions that followers passionately adopt. With a compelling vision that people in the organization embrace, they march in the same direction, much like schools of fish or flocks of birds in flight. Would people have followed Moses for 40 years in the desert without a compelling vision? Would the civil rights movement in the United

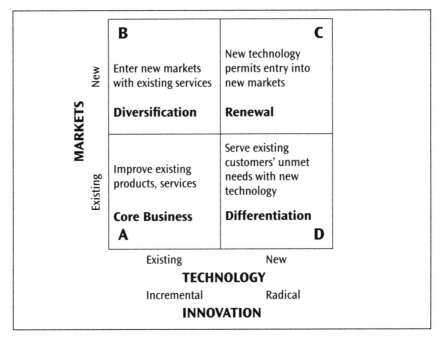

Figure 11-1. Analysis of Resource Allocation to Innovation

States have been as effective without Martin Luther King, Jr.'s compelling "I Have a Dream" speech?

A team can be as small as two people in a company owned by both. The power of vision and mission is still undeniable and can keep the company running when all looks less than rosy.

> **BALANCE RESOURCES**          **SMART**
>
> There needs to be a proper allocation of resources given to incremental innovation and radical innovation in your          **MANAGING**
> team. This balance will be different for every team and every organization, and you need to make a determination about the balance that's proper for your team. Many times the compelling mission/vision will help you make proper resource allocation.

## Example: Krehson Company

Here's an example. Howard Kress and Ed Johnson formed a partnership in 2005 to develop, manufacture, and sell a small helicopter at a price around $15,000. Their compelling vision is spelled in the acronym FIRES, which stands for fun, innovative, reliable, eco-friendly and economical, and safe.

Their design features the stability of two counter-rotating rotors without the need for a tail rotor. Eliminating the tail rotor reduces weight, reduces the machine complexity, and makes it easier to fly the aircraft. Without a tail rotor, however, finding a way to effect a turn (a "yaw" in aeronautical terms) became a challenge. After several false starts, Ed had an idea: if lift were increased on one rotor and simultaneously decreased on the other counter-rotating rotor by the same amount, a torque imbalance would occur, effecting the desired turn, with no waste of power. The "lift shift" was solved by placing small flaps on the trailing edge of each blade and controlling them appropriately. Neither Howard nor Ed had ever seen such an arrangement, and their patent search online revealed nothing similar.

Their excitement was electric! They set about putting their idea into practice by building a small prototype helicopter. Tests of the prototype demonstrated immediate precise control of yaw. To name their invention, they reasoned that since flaps on airplanes are called *ailerons* and changing the direction of flight is called *yaw*, the name would be

"Yawlerons." Their patent attorney discovered no filing for any similar system. On February 22, 2007, the U.S. Patent and Trademark Office issued a Notice of Publication of Application number 11/678044.

The financial impact of the poor economy caused them to suspend work on the helicopter in the fall of 2008. However, they had previously worked on an ultralight ground vehicle that they decided to resurrect. The target specifications are 55-mph maximum speed, 150 mpg on gasoline, and reasonable cargo space. Certainly their performance specifications are a challenge that most automotive engineers would laugh at. But performance tests are under way, and the results are very encouraging.

The energizing aspect of this wildly optimistic challenge is 100 percent involvement by dedicated people who are targeted by their vision—FIRES. Howard said, "Our faith in each other and in our FIRES vision of a strong organization producing excellent machines for business and pleasure enable us to continue, even in the face of intimidating circumstances." I have a feeling that we will be seeing Krehson air and land vehicles (*www.krehsonpuv.com*) available in due course.

**SMART**

**MANAGING**

## Inspire Toward a Greater Good, a Higher Purpose

The most compelling missions/visions are *not* about money, but rather about a greater good and a higher purpose. Take, for example, President John F. Kennedy's vision in 1961 that "this nation should commit itself to achieving the goal, before this decade is out, of landing a man on the moon and returning him safely to the earth," or a research manager's vision that "We are giving your Mother back her freedom every day" when he wanted to motivate people to develop adult incontinence products.

## Example: Hoffman, LLC

An outstanding example comes from Hoffman, LLC, in Appleton, Wisconsin. Paul J. Hoffman is the fourth generation of a general construction company founded in 1892. Paul's father was a left-brained civil engineer and expected his son to be the same. However, Paul was a right-brained dreamer. He graduated with a degree in psychology, not engineering.

In 1977 his father called him and said, "It's time to join the family business." Reluctantly Paul joined the company. In his first week, he was amazed to discover that a 2 x 4 did not really measure 2"x 4"!

Only two months later, his father announced, "I'm retiring. Take over." Paul politely said, "No, thank you." Instead, Paul formed a new company and also took on the responsibility of closing the 85-year-old family business. Paul's innovative idea in 1977 was to take total responsibility for building projects, beginning with the clients' vision about the kind of building they wanted, and managing the whole process through to completion with a fully integrated project delivery method. Only 2 of the 200 employees from the family business had the courage to join Paul in his unproven, innovative, and highly unconventional venture.

By 1994 the 17-year-old company had grown to 20 employees. Paul had created an innovative firm unlike any other, but he felt something was missing—a true purpose.

Paul assembled his employees and asked them to each write the epitaph they wanted to see on their gravestones. The skeptical group wrote their epitaphs. Surprisingly, not one included the words "work," "job," "career," "money," or "wealth."

He asked, "Why do we work?" The consensus was that work was to earn a living, not create their epitaphs. Paul then asked them to name the company's 10 most successful projects. The list contained a church, a domestic abuse shelter, a retirement housing project, a school, etc. When he asked why these projects made the list, it was obvious that every one of these buildings enhanced the lives of the people who benefited from them, and that none of the projects was listed because it was built on time and on budget or it was highly profitable.

Paul proclaimed that this simple exercise proved that Hoffman was an important and fulfilling part of their life's purpose. Everyone believed it and bought in. The entire company contributed to develop the company's mission: "We make a positive impact on people's lives and their environment by providing creative ideas and responsible solutions." In this case, the company's mission is also its compelling challenge. From that point on, Hoffman became a mission-driven company with a consistent guiding purpose.

The mission was (and still is) front and center. Paul and his employees defined the mission, developed a set of guiding principles for their culture and their work, continually communicated the mission, and built the company and its decisions around it. In three short years, the company grew from 20 to 100-plus employees with revenues exceeding $100 million. The company named its unique, integrated project delivery process "Total Project Management" and developed a cartoon to creatively differentiate the company from competitors. It also redefined the word "environment" in its mission. It began to implement sustainable (green) practices into their projects, because the mission demanded it, not because it was "the thing to do."

The year 2000 began a series of roller-coaster rides for Hoffman. Since Paul had an interest in several other businesses and had taken on many civic activities, he appointed a senior manager as president. Unfortunately, the company's economic health deteriorated. As a result, in 2001 Paul returned as president.

Seeking a solution to the company's dire situation, Paul creatively leveraged the family's 109-year legacy to rebuild the culture, provide stability, and create a strategic direction for Hoffman. He chose his Great Grandfather Fred as the icon for an initiative named "109 Days with Fred." The focus was on revitalizing, energizing, and renewing the company in 109 days. Throughout that summer, Paul and his employees transformed the company and accomplished what most thought to be impossible, while making it memorable and fun.

On the 108th day, all gathered to celebrate, share successes, and tell stories. To memorialize "109 Days with Fred," Paul declared the Friday before Labor Day (the 109th day) as "Fred Day," a company-paid holiday.

Then, in April 2003, public school projects totaling $100 million failed their referenda on election day and then, over a six-week period, $80 million of additional Hoffman projects were postponed or eliminated. These two practically simultaneous events resulted in a 90 percent reduction in contracted business, which threatened to sink the company.

Paul reached out to a friend who led a large construction company in St. Louis and suggested forming a new company. Hoffman would contribute 100 percent of its company, and the St. Louis partner would contribute cash equal to the value of that 100 percent contribution. Six weeks later, Hoffman, LLC, was born. When the St. Louis company needed a new corporate headquarters, with Hoffman's assistance, its highly sustainable building was recognized by the U.S. Green Building Council as the highest Certified LEED (Leadership in Energy and Environmental Design) Platinum building in the world.

Since Paul was continuing his outside business and civic interests, in early 2005, at the suggestion of his partner, a new president was appointed to Hoffman, LLC. Again, sadly, a contrast in management style changed the corporate culture, innovation was not encouraged, and the company's financial performance did not match the overstated financial projections from management.

In January 2007, Paul acquired full ownership of the company, only to find the financial situation far worse than anticipated. Paul immediately held an all-employee meeting to share the disheartening news and announce his two primary goals: rebuild and perpetuate the company and help every employee become a leader and the best version of himself or herself. With conviction, Paul said that by staying true to the mission with focus and discipline, the company would survive.

"I imagined I was on the Titanic," he explains, "and had only one lifeboat for 20 people. I had to choose 20 of the 73 passengers that gave us the best chance for survival." He met individually with each of the 20 and asked them each to choose the occupants of their own "lifeboat," without any capacity restriction. They had 24 hours to decide. The next day, Paul received 19 "lifeboat lists" and one letter of resignation. He discovered that 18 of the current employees were on nobody's list. Immediately, Paul helped the 18 leave gracefully and find other jobs.

To flatten the corporate hierarchy, he chose a group of 10 "captains," many of whom had little leadership experience. Each captain was to be the leader of a specific area of the company. The company cut expenses, closed an office, and moved its headquarters, which saved the company over $2 million annually. To the remaining employees, he said, "We are going to change the paradigm of growth used in our industry. At Hoffman, growth will be measured in our heads, hearts, and wallets. Profit will be measured by profit per employee. We will connect our company to other organizations that will increase our revenue, capabilities, capacity, and benefit from our project delivery process and sustainable intellectual capital."

Throughout all the turmoil, Hoffman's mission has been its beacon of light, purpose, focus, and direction. Today the company is profitable, true to its mission, respectful of its legacy (Fred Day remains a corporate holiday), grooming future leaders for succession who fully embody the mission and Paul's "people first" approach, continuously sharing information, and ever maintaining a climate for creativity and innovation.

**SMART**

**MANAGING**

**MAKE YOUR MISSION MATTER**
A compelling mission can inspire employees and managers to achieve great heights and survive severe lows. Paul said, "We absolutely would not have survived as a company had we not remained true to the original mission. It continues to serve us today. Those 18 words are our guiding light for future generations."

Again and again we see the overriding importance of the leadership in providing a compelling organizational or business *challenge* and building *trust and openness*, which results in higher levels of independent action (*risk taking*), providing a forum and time for ideas to emerge (*idea time*), and then finding ways to give new ideas an early try at low cost (*idea support*). Gone are the natural barriers created by functional organizational structures, turf battles, and—the most sinister of all—zero-sum performance rating systems that pit employees against each other for a limited number of "good" ratings, thereby ensuring competition among people and groups rather than cooperation.

## Lead Change

A synonym for "innovation" is "change." There can be no innovation, incremental or radical, without some degree of change, and the leader must absolutely lead change before anyone else will follow. When we speak of becoming a leader of innovation, we also mean becoming a leader of change.

Everyone has a preferred orientation to change, determined more by genetics than by situation (Chapter 12). People who are *agents of stability* will favor change that is incremental, whereas people who are *agents of change* will favor change that is more radical.

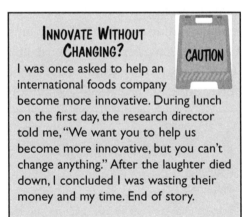

**KEY LEARNING FROM HOFFMAN, LLC**

Paul's plan to keep the company healthy when he no longer is in charge is to ensure that successors embody and live his fundamental beliefs about leadership:

1. Leadership is never about ego and power; it's about helping people to better themselves beyond even their own beliefs.
2. You can't share too much information with others.
3. You can't share too much of the leadership with others.
4. You can't share too much of the successes, and you can't give too much credit to others.
5. You can't promote the mission too much. Constantly keep it in front of everyone.

In companies like Hoffman, LLC, we see very strong parallels between the validated dimensions of the climate for innovation and the climate that the leaders of the company have consciously set. Paul Hoffman works hard to ensure that the natural barriers to creativity and innovation that appear in more traditionally run organizations never have a chance to develop. This is our challenge for leaders at every level—removing barriers to creativity and innovation and then working to keep barriers from developing.

If you find yourself leading a team with a mission of incremental innovation and you are a strong agent of change naturally preferring radical innovation, you will be able to do a great job so long as you are willing to expend the *coping energy* (Chapter 12) necessary to lead the team in the way that is consistent with its mission. Similarly, if you

**INNOVATE WITHOUT CHANGING?** CAUTION

I was once asked to help an international foods company become more innovative. During lunch on the first day, the research director told me, "We want you to help us become more innovative, but you can't change anything." After the laughter died down, I concluded I was wasting their money and my time. End of story.

are a strong agent of stability leading a team with a mission of radical innovation, you will need to adjust your leadership style to match the team's mission or the team will likely be unsuccessful. If the adjustments require too much coping energy on your part, you would do well to find an assignment that better matches your preferred style.

**KEY TERMS**

**Agent of Stability** A person who prefers to perfect the system, favors change that is incremental, and perceives of problems as opportunities to make an existing system work better, faster, or cheaper.

**Agent of Change** A person who prefers to change the system, favors change that is more radical, and perceives of problems as opportunities to develop new processes or systems and create new products or services to meet unarticulated needs of customers.

# Create a Self-Sustaining Culture of Innovation

The climate for innovation (Chapter 10) mirrors physics in that systems tend to move toward their lowest energy state. That's why water runs downhill, springs tend to unwind, and the climate for innovation tends to get worse when supportive leaders leave. In nature, it takes a restraining force to keep water from running downhill or a big enough pump to get it back up the hill. In organizations, it takes the same sort of dedication and consistent attention to be sure the climate for innovation remains healthy. It takes dedication and hard work on the part of the leader to ensure that the climate for innovation isn't the first victim when a business downturn occurs. Consequently, it's necessary to pay consistent attention to the health of the dimensions of the climate for innovation in order to make it self-sustaining.

**SMART MANAGING**

**IMPORTANCE OF ORIENTATION**

Team members will be more effective, less stressed, and happier in jobs that require the same orientation to change that they themselves prefer. Likewise, leaders will be more effective when they lead initiatives that are consistent with their own orientation to change. This means that the successful quality manager shouldn't be put in charge of innovation and the successful innovation manager shouldn't be made the leader of a Six Sigma effort.

To make innovation self-sustaining, it must become one of your company's values, rooted in its beliefs about itself and its business. That is, innovation must become a part of your company's culture. True organizational values are revealed during the budgeting process when hard choices have to be made among competing values. Innovative organizations make choices that favor innovation instead of only short-term profit objectives, so budgeting is a good place to start. Changing the organizational culture does not happen overnight; it takes a long time with continued attention and effort—and a transformational leader.

I like to think of the mental model of the transformational leader as shown in Figure 11-2. Note that values for innovation are always intangibles and represent the "management talk." Note also that the three supporting items are tangibles that reflect the "management walk." The desired culture can become reality only when the management talk is reflected in the management walk—when managers do what they say they will do. We can say that a culture values innovation only if and because managers support innovation through their behavior, as shown in Figure 11-2.

The three areas of tangible behavior are

1. recognition,
2. elimination of negative behavior,
3. regular repetitive events.

Recognition for those who deliver innovative results lies at the heart of building intrinsic motivation. What innovators really want is recognition of their work and some autonomy to continue it. When recognizing people, you will want to recognize their competence, ability, loyalty, and commitment. These words of recognition reinforce the positive self-concept, and people want to achieve even more. Intrinsic motivation is increased, and people set very challenging goals that are more likely to result in additional breakthroughs.

Negative behavior that undermines the value for innovation must be eliminated. Examples of such negative behavior would include the following:

- Interpersonal conflict among team members
- Managers taking credit for the ideas of their people without attribution
- Instantly judging ideas negatively
- Withholding support and resources

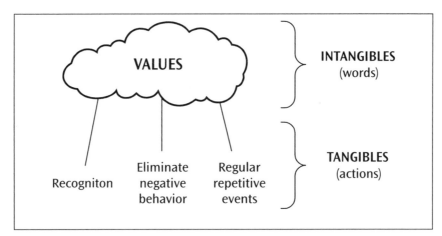

**Figure 11-2.** Mental model of the transformational leader

### Tricks of the Trade

### GOOD LEADERS MAKE RECOGNITION PERSONAL

If you have ever received a *handwritten* note of congratulations and recognition from your boss, there is a **95** percent chance you still have that note tucked away in a special place. People don't throw away these personal notes because such displays of recognition build and re-inforce their self-esteem, and they'll always have a warm feeling toward leaders who express recognition personally.

The magic of handwriting shouts that the boss appreciates and values you enough to take the time to handwrite a special note to you. With the growth of e-mail, hardly anyone sends handwritten notes anymore, so grab your pen and try writing notes of thanks to especially deserving people. You will be amazed at the response. Although better than nothing, e-mail cannot convey the depth of your personal appreciation and thanks to the recipient.

You can make a handwritten note of recognition more effective by sending it to the person's home address. This makes the person a hero in his or her own household, and you will always be remembered very warmly for it. People who have experienced this kind of recognition always say that it makes them want to achieve even more ... and no money accompanied this recognition.

- Habitually falling into one of the five pitfalls described in Chapter 2

The problem with attempting to eliminate negative behavior is that the effort usually causes pain for the offender and confrontation for the leader, and most people would rather not be a party to a confrontational event. Eliminating negative behavior takes courage and commitment.

Regular repetitive events could consist of adding 10 minutes to your staff meeting to discuss innovative ideas, perhaps teaching a creativity technique, perhaps recognizing a team member for some innovative approach. A number of companies hold annual "innovation fairs" at which poster sessions display innovative activities under way within the company, possibly in the cafeteria for all to see. You might consider an annual "innovation day" during which important innovations are highlighted and the innovators are made corporate heroes with recognition.

> ### PROMOTE STORIES OF INNOVATION
>
> **SMART MANAGING**
>
> The 3M Co. produced a small handbook called *Innovation Chronicles* that succinctly captured major 3M innovations with stories of discovery, development, and commercialization. This little handbook elevated the innovators to the status of corporate heroes. This booklet, freely given to prospective employees, underscores the value that 3M places on innovation. The organization becomes the stories it tells! Follow the example of 3M: tell stories of innovation to create role models of your innovators and to underscore the value of innovation to your organization.

> ### SAFETY OR ELSE
>
> **FOR EXAMPLE**
>
> Air Products and Chemicals, Inc., of Allentown, Pennsylvania, is well known for its stellar safety performance, having been named the safest chemical company in the world in 2007 and 2008, overtaking DuPont for the first time in history. Negative behavior in regard to safety will be absolutely driven from the company. A phrase sometimes heard goes something like "You will work safely here, or you will work somewhere else."

# Manager's Checklist for Chapter 11

☑ Develop a social contract with your team as a prerequisite for working to improve the climate for innovation.

☑ The climate for innovation matters more than superficial material trappings of the workplace.

☑ Treat "mistakes" as opportunities to learn, rather than opportunities to blame and punish. Hold people who have made mistakes accountable to share what they have learned so that the entire team benefits.

☑ A compelling mission/vision is the best way to achieve team alignment.

☑ You must become the leader of innovation (change) if you expect team members to follow.

☑ Create a self-sustaining culture of innovation through your actions to recognize innovative behavior, eliminate negative behavior, and sponsor repetitive events to keep innovation visible to everyone.

☑ Tell stories of innovation that have occurred in your organization as well as within your team. Consider preparing a booklet to promote the stories of innovation in your company.

# Getting the Right People into the Right Jobs

P robably no other subject is more poorly understood, yet more critically important, than getting the right people into the right jobs. This is true not only for innovation, but for every aspect of the job and career. When people are in jobs they love, job satisfaction improves, productivity increases, and absenteeism and turnover decrease.

Jobs are all about problem solving. Every living organism solves problems; bees find flowers to pollinate, birds build nests to cradle their eggs that contain the next generation, and we all solve a myriad of problems as we live our lives, whether at home, socially, or at work. We all use our creativity in solving problems. How we tend to do this is a reflection of our innate preferred style of creativity or problem-solving style. This is that inborn orientation to problem solving that leads some of us to be *agents of stability*, preferring to perfect the existing system, and others of us to be *agents of change*, preferring to change the existing system.

I feel sure that what you learn in this chapter about problem-solving style and its many implications will remain with you forever. Use of these concepts will help you form stronger, more effective teams. You will be able to use what you learn here on the job to make better hiring decisions so that you hire the people most likely to fit well with the job. You will be able to use what you learn here to better diagnose performance issues when poor performance is a result of poor job fit. You will be able to form stronger working alliances among people who normally might have a difficult time working productively with each other.

I will be describing a framework of cognitive style as applied to problem solving—that is, how people prefer to use their creativity as they solve problems. This was first described by Dr. Michael Kirton in his Adaption-Innovation Theory (*Adaptors and Innovators: Styles of Creativity and Problem Solving,* London: Routledge, 1989.) This is a framework that you intuitively already understand, and the concept is so very simple that you will wonder why you never quite put it all together before. This understanding will change your life, and you will see why people tend to gravitate to certain types of work or to aspects of their assigned jobs while ignoring the rest. It will help you design effective strategies to improve the working environment for all, reducing turnover through improving job satisfaction.

# Jobs Are All About Solving Problems

Different people solve problems in different ways. When you have the right people in the right positions, they prosper and so does the organization. You enhance the potential for innovation by matching skills, aptitudes, and personalities with the right tasks. Let's look more at this.

## A Success Story About Style

John is a real guy whose name I have changed. He was failing in his job as a research chemist in one of DuPont's laboratories where I was a research manager. John holds a Ph.D. in physical chemistry, and I greatly admired his intellectual abilities. When John was moved into my group, it was a last-ditch attempt to save his career. For the preceding three years, John had been assigned the job of developing innovative new chemistries that would improve one of DuPont's fiber products. He was failing to make much headway. In so many words, I was told to "fix him or fire him."

During our first interview, I asked John a simple question that would change his life: "Tell me something you did or accomplished in high school that made you feel good about yourself." He didn't hesitate. In a very excited voice, he said that he had played trumpet in the band, which was totally dysfunctional. Nobody was keeping track of the band fees—"We didn't know who owed how much and the music was in such disarray we could hardly find it when needed." So John saw the need for a secretary to the band; he created the position and appointed himself. He created a system to account for band fees and for effi-

**MOST VALUABLE RESOURCE**

John's story reveals an important point about organizations and innovation. Your most valuable resource is not the people. It's *the right people in the right jobs!*

**SMART MANAGING**

ciently organizing and filing the music. During the graduation ceremony, after all the diplomas had been handed out, the principal called him up on the stage and presented him with a plaque honoring his contributions to the band. Very excited, he added, "I still have it!"

It was clear that John was in the wrong job. He obviously preferred jobs that let him perfect the system, bringing order out of chaos and making everything work as well as possible. We members of management very naïvely thought that a person with a Ph.D. in a science would be gifted at creating new products or services, changing the system rather than perfecting it. This is a false assumption, which led us to make the wrong assignment for John, and we were about to fire him for our mistake.

But this story has a happy ending. It so happened that there was a job opening in our plant where we needed bright people like John to keep our processes running well, making the highest-quality product possible day after day—in other words, perfecting the manufacturing system. John was offered the job, which he quickly accepted. That move was such a success that John's career flourished and he is still with DuPont!

John is now in the right job. Who won? Everyone of course! John won: he got a good job he loves that allowed him to stay with a great company. DuPont won: the company kept a great employee, properly assigned. The customers also won because the energy that John was wasting trying to cope with a job that was not right for him is now going into work that benefits from his problem-solving style, ultimately giving the customers a better product at a lower price.

Finding a job that matched John's preferred problem-solving style was the key to changing poor performance to excellent and making an unhappy employee content. I will have more tips on how you might apply this concept a little later.

People naturally fall on the continuum between the extremes of perfecting and changing the system, and Figure 12-1 shows this continuum from left to right. At the left extreme are those who prefer to perfect the existing system (agents of stability), like John, and at the right extreme are those who prefer to change the existing system (agents of change). In the center are those whose style is flexible and can therefore more easily shift their behavior from one side to the other as a particular job or assignment might require.

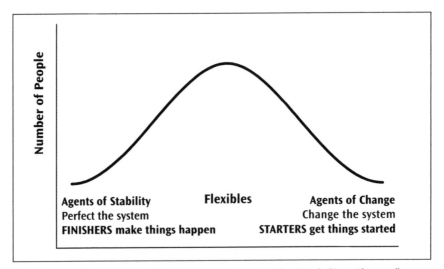

**Figure 12-1.** Histogram of the population along the "Stability–Change" Continuum

People who prefer to perfect the system—that is, agents of stability—see problems as opportunities to make an existing system work better, faster, or cheaper. These people tend to be very detail-oriented, they're reliable and responsible, and they deliver on commitments. You don't have a functioning business without people who approach problem solving in this way. Without people who are agents of stability, products might not get produced on time, invoices might not get written and sent, bills might not get paid, and paychecks might not get written. These jobs usually require people behaving in ways that perfect the system.

By contrast, people who prefer to change the system—that is, agents of change—see problems as opportunities to develop new processes or

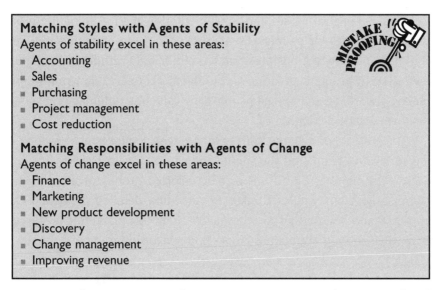

**Matching Styles with Agents of Stability**
Agents of stability excel in these areas:
- Accounting
- Sales
- Purchasing
- Project management
- Cost reduction

**Matching Responsibilities with Agents of Change**
Agents of change excel in these areas:
- Finance
- Marketing
- New product development
- Discovery
- Change management
- Improving revenue

systems and create new products or services to meet the unarticulated needs of customers.

Agents of change find ways to improve work processes or systems, usually by creating a new process or system, as opposed to repairing or improving the existing one. You don't have a functioning long-term business without people who prefer to use their creativity as they solve problems in this way.

The following explains problem-solving styles beautifully. You will be able to start using this understanding in your job the minute you put this book down.

# Job Demand for Problem-Solving Style

Job demand for problem-solving style is the kind of behavior that a particular job might require in order to do it well. For example, accounting jobs require handling details with great accuracy, whereas marketing jobs require an intuitive feel for what will appeal to potential customers.

Clearly some jobs require behavior that tends to perfect the system (accounting, digging for details, critical thinking), while others require behavior that tends to change the system (new products and services, seeing the bigger picture, innovative thinking). On an innovation team, the people who are naturally agents of stability tend to contribute more to fixing existing processes and implementation than to initiating new projects, whereas the people who are naturally agents of change tend to start new initiatives. A business that has either style without the other is ineffective at bringing anything new to the marketplace. However, when both styles are present and all people truly value the differences in style, the team will be dynamite!

The critical point is that both styles are required for a high-performing, innovative team, and you should strive to find team assignments for each team member that fit his or her preferred problem-solving style. Don't assign your wildest thinker to providing detailed data for EPA approval, and don't assign your best accountant to a marketing position. Both will be unhappy and quit. Worse, both will be unhappy and not quit.

---

### EACH STYLE WITH ITS STRENGTHS

**FOR EXAMPLE**

When Jack Johnson was the internal management consultant at the Smithsonian Institution, one of the senior leaders revealed that she was exasperated with one of her subordinates, who was not performing a task assigned to her six months earlier. The supervisor had asked her employee to develop a new process for archiving electronic information. She did not understand why this normally hard-working, seasoned member of the team had not completed the assignment.

Jack understood their problem-solving styles. He knew that the supervisor was strongly an agent of change, a big-picture thinker, able to see new opportunities and be more visionary, while her subordinate was strongly an agent of stability, able to implement plans, improve processes, and deliver on commitments, but not gifted at creating new processes.

This information enabled the supervisor to understand that she and her subordinate could collaborate on this project. The supervisor created a framework for the new process, and the subordinate filled in the gaps and the details and produced the desired outcome!

The problem completely disappeared once both saw the value that each other's style could bring to the job. When both were working in their preferred styles, they performed very well as an innovative team!

---

## Recognizing a Person's Style

You may be wondering how you can tell an employee's problem-solving style. There are a number of ways. Probably the most direct way is to observe how the person behaves and how he or she has performed on different kinds of jobs and, of course, to ask questions.

A person is almost certainly an agent of stability if he or she

- plans well with detailed lists made for most everything;
- is highly detail-oriented;
- has a few good ideas that are more incremental than disruptive or radical;
- generally works within the rules (standard operating procedures) to meet expectations;
- is reliable, responsible, and predictable.

A person is almost certainly an agent of change if he or she

- is generally more spontaneous, maybe even impulsive, and less likely to plan;
- is better at seeing the "big picture" than focusing on the details;
- tends to have a great many ideas that are more disruptive or radical than incremental;
- believes that rules are at best suggestions, not necessarily meant for him or her;
- is entrepreneurial and visionary.

The excellent work by Greg Stevens and Kurt Swogger in three articles in *Research-Technology Management* ("Creating a Winning R&D Culture – I & II," Vol. 52, Nos. 1 & 2, 2009 and "Piloting the Rocket of Radical Innovation," Vol. 46, No. 2, 2003) deserves special mention. Using the very well-known and widely used Myers-Briggs Type Indicator (M.B.T.I.®) of psychological type, Stevens developed his Rainmaker Indexsm (RI) using M.B.T.I.® data from team

**UNDERSTAND PEOPLE BETTER**

There are instruments that will help you better understand your team members **TOOLS** and their problem-solving orientations:

- Team Dimensions Profile (formerly Innovate with CARE), available from *www.corexcel.com/care*
- Orchid Module, available from *www.imaginatik.com*
- Herrmann Brain Dominance Instrument®, available from *www.hbdi.com*
- Myers-Briggs Type Indicator (M.B.T.I.®) and the KAI Inventory widely available through certified consultants.

members and showed bottom-line business value by using the RI to properly place team members in innovation assignments that suited their type. Stevens and Swogger coined the terms "starters" and "finishers," and when the terms were properly assigned, the authors documented an increase of $23 billion in cumulative value between 1991 and 2008 in a formerly commoditized plastics business at the Dow Chemical Company.

## Orientation vs. Behavior

Matters of individual orientation are generally thought to be inborn and not changeable, like your eye color: it picked you, you didn't pick it, and you cannot choose to change it. Your preferred style of problem solving is an inborn orientation: it came with you at birth, and it does not change.

However, behavior is always situational, and you are in charge—you can choose to change your behavior to match the demands of any particular situation. If you happen to have blue eyes and you want to appear to have brown eyes, you can simply wear brown contact lenses. Others will see you as having brown eyes, but of course your natural eye color hasn't changed. Your natural eye color is like your problem-solving orientation—it will not change—but just as you can change your perceived eye color through the contact lenses you can change your behavior as demanded by the situation.

# Jobs on a Continuum

Jobs can be placed on the same problem-solving style continuum that I have been describing for people, with stability to the left and change to the right. I like to call it the *"job demand for problem-solving style."*

## Finance and Accounting

If asked on which side of the continuum the job of accounting and finance would appear, most people would say the jobs fall on the left of the continuum, because these jobs require that people pay attention to details and work within established rules and methods. They would be partially correct.

Yes, accounting tasks lie on the left of the continuum, but finance tasks lie on the right of the continuum, where people must be more innovative about finding new sources of financing, seeking to change the system. Yet in most companies there is one position titled, "Senior Vice President of Accounting and Finance." That person will naturally gravitate toward the function of the job (either finance or accounting) that most closely matches his or her preferred style. That's because it's easier and more fun, and people tend to gravitate to the jobs that are easier and more fun.

It is much better to split the job in two, with a senior vice president of accounting and a senior vice president of finance, and put someone with the appropriate orientation in each function. (This exact approach is being taken by LuriteK, Inc. *www.luritek.com*, based on this understanding.) However, if the senior vice president is leading an accounting and finance team, he or she must be aware of the need for different problem-solving styles and hire and assign team members to the functions that best fit their style.

---

## PENNY WISE, POUND FOOLISH

**FOR EXAMPLE**

The CFO of a defense contractor in Maryland suddenly realized the huge mistake he had made when he reassigned his best accountant to a finance position. When he learned about problem-solving orientation and the continuum of job demand for problem-solving style, he said, "That explains the huge mistake I just made!"

Although she was a highly successful accountant, she was struggling in the finance job because she was trying to get everything to balance to the nearest penny! He told her that it was just finance and rounding off to the nearest $100,000 would be quite all right. "I can't do that," she said. "It has to balance to the nearest penny!"

He realized he had set her up for failure, since there was no way she could do well in that job. He decided then and there to move her back to her accounting position, which made her very happy, and he was then able to find the right person for the finance position.

---

## Sales and Marketing

How about the problem-solving styles demanded by sales and marketing? Marketing naturally falls on the right of the continuum because it's about creating demand for your products and services, whereas sales naturally falls on the left because it involves delivering the goods, keeping track of the sales data, and helping with production planning. Yet most businesses have one person in charge of both, as Senior Vice President of Sales and Marketing.

**SYSTEM SAVES CAREER**

**FOR EXAMPLE**

Walter Finkelstein, currently CEO of the Deep Learning Group of Rockville, Maryland, heard me speak at a meeting of CEOs and phoned me the next day after my presentation. Walt said, "I can't thank you enough! The insight I gained helped me save the job of one of my valued key executives! I was going to fire him the afternoon you spoke. Instead, I explained this system to him; we both instantly recognized the job he was doing was not right for him because it required him to use too much of his energy just coping. Using my new knowledge, I found the right job for this man, his career was saved, and that's worth more than money."

**SMART**

**MANAGING**

**TWO GREAT QUESTIONS!**

In an article titled "What God Made Us Good At" (*Newsweek*, October 12, 2005), Rabbi Marc Gellman made a strong point that we are happiest when we are doing what God made us good at. You might ask, "When am I most happy?" Great question! You are always most happy when you're doing what you love, and what you love is always what God made you good at. This question is worth discussing with current or potential members of your team.

The other great question is the one that I asked John, the DuPont research chemist: "Tell me about one of your accomplishments that you enjoyed doing and made you feel good about yourself." Listen for the underlying characteristics that were so satisfying, and then determine which jobs might have similar characteristics. You might find a perfect fit for an employee struggling in a job that's sapping coping energy.

After the CEO of a company in Appleton, Wisconsin, learned about problem-solving styles and the job demand continuum, he remarked, "That explains why I have such a lousy marketing department! Our marketing department really stinks!" He said, "We hire people into sales positions and, if they do really well (which means it fits them), we promote them into marketing, and they don't do very well. They languish there doing a so-so job, but we're too nice—we don't return people to a lower level and don't usually fire anyone." Since he owned the business, he had the freedom to create a progression system in sales that did not require moving over to marketing, and in marketing, people no longer had to come from sales.

If you happen to be facing a surgery, would you prefer your surgeon behave on the left, perfecting the system, or on the right, changing the system? Most people would want their surgeons to behave on the left, perfecting the system and returning their ailing body to a state of wellness. It's not the time for a research project when you are on the operating room table! In fact, all our medical professionals are required to behave on the left of the scale, using FDA-prescribed procedures and drugs. I am reminded of a cartoon that shows several brain surgeons gathered around a poor patient on the operating room table. The patient's leg has sprung into the air, and one surgeon tells the others something like "Poke his brain right where I have my finger!" The surgeons are behaving on the right of the scale, experimenting with a poor patient, when in fact you intuitively expect the surgeon to behave on the left of the scale, returning the systems to normal.

---

### FROM PRACTICE TO RESEARCH

**FOR EXAMPLE**

Kevin Streete of Bowie, Maryland, earned his MD degree at the urging of his parents. However, he was totally unhappy as a practicing physician and hated going to work, although he did not fully understand why. Kevin was one of my students in an Executive MBA class on innovation at the University of Maryland in early 2009. There he learned that his problem-solving style was exactly opposite the style required to be a practicing physician.

"This was the most eye-opening thing I ever learned about myself," he said. "It explains everything. For the first time I truly understand why I dislike working as a physician so much, and why I liked research jobs in the past. I am going to find a job in medical research where I can be truly happy." Incidentally, Kevin is designing a line of women's and men's clothing as a hobby and is considering making this a second career.

---

## Calculating Coping Energy, E = dt

The concept of coping energy was developed by Dr. Michael Kirton as part of his adaption innovation theory, and the stories above illustrate the damage that exerting too much coping energy can do over a long period of time.

Figure 12-2 shows that coping energy is equal to *coping degree* (distance between problem-solving preference and job demand) (d) multiplied by the *time* (t) expected to keep up the behavior.

Coping energy is a costly, zero-value energy drain that contributes nothing to solving problems. It just adds to personal stress. It drains your

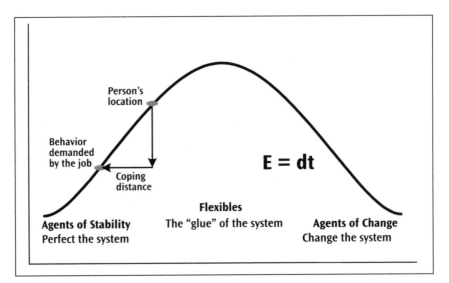

Person's
location

Behavior
demanded
by the job

Coping
distance

E = dt

Flexibles
The "glue" of the system

Agents of Stability
Perfect the system

Agents of Change
Change the system

**Figure 12-2.** Coping Energy = Coping Degree x Time Expected to Continue the Behavior

**KEY TERMS**

**Coping Degree** The difference between the demand of a job and a person's problem-solving style.

**Coping Energy** The product of coping degree multiplied by length of time expected to continue a job. The equation is written as $E = dt$, where $E = $ coping energy, $d = $ coping degree, and $t = $ time expected to continue doing the job.

"energy bucket" so that there is none left to do the work. That's where the stress, the burnout, and the poor job satisfaction come from—trying to do the job when all the energy was wasted in coping.

To help get the right people into the right jobs means finding jobs that minimize the coping degree in order to minimize the coping energy. I firmly believe that our highest calling as leaders is to help each person do well in his or her jobs. Of course, this means providing resources, support, direction, and all the things that we normally think of as good leaders. However, it is equally important to assign team members to jobs that match each member's problem-solving style.

In my classes and workshops, after gaining permission, I ask a participant who's a strong agent of change to role-play with me a little. I will play the boss, and he or she will play one of my employees.

## HIGH COST OF STRESS

Cynthia C. is a talented organizational development and innovation consultant. Even though she is strongly an agent of change, she earned her CPA certification and was very effective as a tax director (agent of stability) for a number of oil companies for almost 20 years. Because she is right-brained and the tax jobs required left-brained activities, she experienced great job stress and expended a great amount of coping energy. The stress of working outside her area of interest and natural strengths resulted in a variety of illnesses. Although Cynthia was very good at her jobs, she just wasn't happy or content because of the mismatch between her problem-solving style and the style that the job demanded.

While we can choose to shift our behavior and decide to cope in a job that does not match our style, the cost of coping over a long period of time will be heavy and health usually suffers. I can't think of a job that is worth losing your health.

Happily, Cynthia has created a consultancy that closely matches her style—and the job stress is gone.

I announce that we've had a problem over the weekend: our cost accountant quit. And I ask this person if he or she would do us the favor of cost accounting for our team for three weeks until I can find a replacement. There is generally a lot of groaning and moaning, since the job of cost accountant requires an agent of stability and it is unsuitable for this person. But the time is short (three weeks), and the person can handle the stress (E = dt) for three weeks. The person might even become mysteriously "ill" or might decide to take vacation. However, being a good team player, the person accepts the job and comes to work every day and does a great job because he or she wants the team to be successful. And being a very insightful leader, I observe this person's good results and conclude that he or she is doing well. I then conclude (wrongly) that this person likes the work and that the job is a good fit! How many times has that happened to you?

Then I fast-forward the role-play. I announce that three weeks have passed, and I tell the participant, "I have good news—you are getting an extra $1,000 in your paycheck this month for the extra work. Congratulations!" Then I add, "And I have even better news. Even though we are going through a downsizing and the job you were doing on the right of the continuum (the one that required the agent of change) is going to be

> ### Good Performance May Hide Bad Fit
> **CAUTION**
> Young people fresh out of school will do most anything in their first job because they want to succeed. Even if the job is not a proper fit for them, they will decide to cope and to do the job as best they know how in order to do well. It is important to be aware that good performance may be the result of excessive coping, which over time will lead to job dissatisfaction and to high turnover.
>
> You will want to have close communication with your people. Ask what parts of the job they like the best and how they might improve their job assignments. Then, listen for disconnects between the job demand and their problem-solving style.

outsourced, you're in luck, because you are now going to be our cost accountant! Isn't that great?"

In terms of our formula, $E = dt$, what I just did to this participant was increase the amount of time, $t$, to an infinite number. The coping distance, $d$, stays the same, very high. Consequently the coping energy suddenly goes extremely high.

## Options for Dealing with Coping Stress

Suppose you find yourself in a situation where coping stress is very high and there doesn't seem to be any end in sight. You have a problem, to say the least. Here are some choices for dealing with that:

1. Quit on the spot (not an option for most people).
2. Look for another job with less coping (the most popular option).
3. "Just do it," as Nike says (the poorest choice of all, as it will ruin your health over a long period).
4. Partner with another employee whose style is different from yours, to cover more of the job responsibilities with greater ease.
5. Restructure the job, bringing it more in line with your style (if you have the authority or the influence to do so).

## Styles on a Team

This issue of coping energy applies to interrelationships on teams as well as it does to the fit between a person and his or her job. For example, have you ever said something like "That person is so easy to work with," or "It's so easy to be with So-and-So"? Those are expressions of the fact that you are close to the other person on the continuum. The coping distance between you and the other person is small, making it easy to develop a good working relationship.

There is an advantage to working with people just like you: it's easy and it's fun! However, bigger than that advantage is the disadvantage that you will miss the benefits of the other type of problem-solving style. For example, if both of you are agents of change, you'll enjoy working with each other, but you will miss deadlines without an agent of stability there to be mindful of the time. On the other hand, if both of you are agents of stability, you will get a lot done, you will plan exceedingly well, and you will not forget details, but you may miss big opportunities without an agent of change there to suggest them.

You can now see the value of selecting a broad range of people with differing problem-solving styles for your team. As a result, the team may take a little longer to get things done, and it may take a little more energy in the beginning for the members to develop working relationships as each agent of change and each agent of stability develops an appreciation for the other style. However, the team will do excellent work.

Dr. Robin Karol, former director of DuPont's Consulting Solutions group, learned the truth of this approach and began assigning people with widely different styles to work on the same project. She says that it took longer, but the output was far better and the quality was recognized as superior by their clients.

## Valuing the Differences in Problem-Solving Style

Even after intellectually accepting that all styles bring value to their businesses and to their teams, people almost always make the mistake of using negative adjectives to describe those unlike themselves. For example, when I ask people to assume they are strong agents of stability ("finishers") and to give me adjectives that describe those who are strong agents of change ("starters"), I get adjectives like "weird," "crazy," "not serious," "head in the clouds," and "unfocused." Then I ask people to do just the opposite, assume they are strong agents of change ("starters") and give me adjectives that describe strong agents of stability ("finish-

> **TRICKS OF THE TRADE**
>
> ### THINK POSITIVE, THINK ADVANTAGES
>
> To start valuing this diversity of problem-solving styles means to think in positive adjectives about what each style can deliver, rather than focus on the negatives. When I think of the positives, I automatically think of what people can do rather than why they should be excluded because of some things they cannot do well. As leader, you may want to post a list of the positive adjectives for each problem-solving style, pointing out the value that each style brings to a team.
>
> Some positive adjectives for agents of stability are "finisher," "reliable," "dependable," "accountable," and "deliver on commitments." Some positive adjectives for agents of change are "starter," "visionary," "entrepreneurial," and "bringing newness and freshness."

ers"), the adjectives I get include "stodgy," "stick in the mud," "pinheads," "dull," and "boring." Then I ask which of these adjectives show true value for the other. Of course, none of them do.

What's happened? Human beings are herding animals. Like cows and fish and birds, we herd with those similar to us, and herds define themselves by those that are excluded. Once the herd has excluded those who are different, the members identify how the outsiders can threaten or damage the herd—and the negative adjectives flow from that. That's what makes it "OK" to discriminate and exclude the outsiders from the business process.

## Making Problem-Solving Style Diversity Work for Your Team

Think of someone with a style very much like your own. Then think of someone whose style is very much unlike yours. Next, think about your perception of the level of competence of each. People who are like you and whom you believe to be competent can easily become your friends: you share information, ask for their advice, perhaps even socialize with them outside of work. People who are unlike you whom you see as highly competent will certainly have your admiration and respect, but it is less likely you will become close personal friends.

Teams function well when the members see each other in either of the top two quadrants in Figure 12-3. However, teams will be quite dysfunctional if the members see each other as not competent and therefore to be

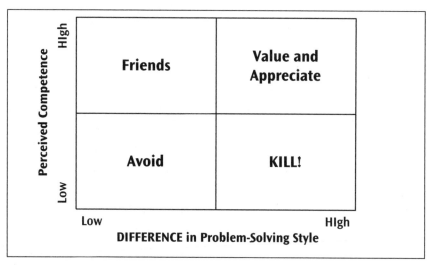

Figure 12-3. Functional teams operate only in the top two quadrants

placed in either of the bottom two quadrants.

# Manager's Checklist for Chapter 12

☑ Problem-solving styles lie along a continuum from *perfecting* the system on the left to *changing* the system on the right.

☑ Everyone is born with a preferred problem-solving style; this orientation is not a matter of choice and doesn't change.

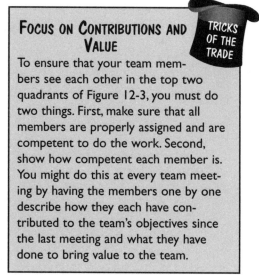

**FOCUS ON CONTRIBUTIONS AND VALUE**

To ensure that your team members see each other in the top two quadrants of Figure 12-3, you must do two things. First, make sure that all members are properly assigned and are competent to do the work. Second, show how competent each member is. You might do this at every team meeting by having the members one by one describe how they each have contributed to the team's objectives since the last meeting and what they have done to bring value to the team.

☑ Specific jobs can be placed along the same continuum in terms of what they demand.

☑ Coping energy must be expended to do a job to the degree of distance between the location of the job demand on the continuum and the location of the person's style on the continuum.

- ☑ Expending high coping energy over a long period of time leads to job stress and poor job satisfaction and contributes to high employee turnover.
- ☑ Helping people find jobs that are right for them means helping them find jobs that reasonably match their orientation so that coping energy is minimized.
- ☑ Improve team functionality by making sure that each each team member is competent to do the work assigned to him or her and that all members see each of the others as competent and adding value to the team!

# Coaching for Innovation

This book has been about helping you foster creativity and innovation among your team members. We have discussed the process and the tools for creative and innovative thinking, setting the climate for innovation, the four tasks of leading innovation, and getting the right people in the right roles for innovation.

Now it is time to tell you about a leadership style we call *coach leader* that you may wish to adopt as you foster creativity and innovation in your team. This chapter will help you transform your leadership style to the coach leader style that will enable team members to exceed even their own expectations for being creative and innovative. Throughout the stories presented in this chapter, you will see recurring leadership themes you may wish to adopt and you will also be given specific things you can begin doing that will help you become a coach leader.

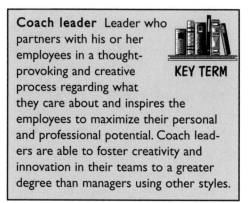

**Coach leader** Leader who partners with his or her employees in a thought-provoking and creative process regarding what they care about and inspires the employees to maximize their personal and professional potential. Coach leaders are able to foster creativity and innovation in their teams to a greater degree than managers using other styles.

**KEY TERM**

This chapter was written by Jack W. Johnson. (See end of chapter for more about author.)

The characteristics and behaviors of a coach leader include the following.

A coach leader helps employees discover for themselves new solutions to problems/issues.

- Is curious in powerful conversations.
- Allows employees freedom to do the work.
- Gives time and support for new ideas.
- Allows employees to be experts and have the answers.
- Allows employees to try new ideas and take risks.
- Helps employees shift their views to see new possibilities.
- Asks powerful questions that help shift how employees think and see issues.
- Can challenge employees and their assessments of issues.
- Evokes inquiry and clarity on issues.

A coach leader creates trusting, open, and intimate relationships.

- Involves employees in powerful conversations regarding issues.
- Creates opportunities for ongoing learning.
- Demonstrates concern for employees and their points of view.
- Builds trust by being vulnerable in acknowledging not knowing the answers.
- Recognizes employees as experts.
- Understands the history and perspectives of employees.

A coach leader communicates effectively.

- Actively listens, focusing on what employees are saying and not saying.
- Guides employees to reveal their underlying concerns, cares, and issues.
- Integrates and builds on employees' ideas.
- Uses speech acts effectively: requests, declarations, offers, promises, assertions, and assessments.
- Welcomes challenges to his or her assessments.
- Actively listens, mirroring what he or she hears, being fully present in conversations.

A coach leader encourages learning and discovery.

- Encourages self-discovery.
- Creates opportunities for ongoing learning.
- Helps others see new possibilities and move on them.

A coach leader cares and feels passionate about people and the business results.

- Talks about what matters to employees in the business (their passions).
- Enrolls others to their cause in conversations.
- Helps draw out and identify barriers to high performance and effectiveness.
- Commits to excellence and change.

# Flexibility in Leadership Style

Many experts have stated that leadership style is situational. We certainly agree. There are times when behaving as an authoritarian leader is necessary to get the results you need and want. However, for creativity and innovation to thrive, some leadership styles are far more effective than others. Some styles facilitate a working environment that fosters and enables creativity, while others do just the opposite. We will be examining these styles and their effects so that you can decide which leadership style you might find appropriate for fostering creativity and innovation on your team.

# Four Leadership Styles for Creativity and Innovation

Let's consider four leadership styles:

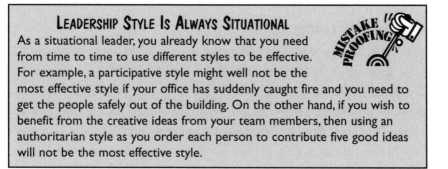

### LEADERSHIP STYLE IS ALWAYS SITUATIONAL

As a situational leader, you already know that you need from time to time to use different styles to be effective. For example, a participative style might well not be the most effective style if your office has suddenly caught fire and you need to get the people safely out of the building. On the other hand, if you wish to benefit from the creative ideas from your team members, then using an authoritarian style as you order each person to contribute five good ideas will not be the most effective style.

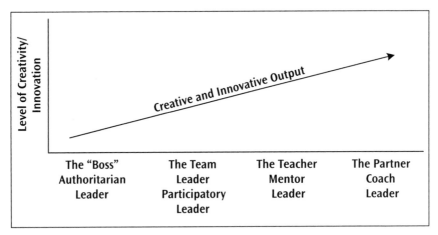

**Figure 13-1.** Leadership style and creative and innovative output

1. Authoritarian leader
2. Participatory leader
3. Mentor leader
4. Coach leader

It is our belief that these four styles lie along a continuum from authoritarian leader to coach leader and the more your behavior reflects those of a coach leader, the more innovative your staff will be. This relationship is diagrammed in Figure 13-1.

## Authoritarian Leader

There are times when it is necessary for a leader to use an authoritarian style and be the "Boss" with a capital "B." This style may be necessary to get something accomplished in a time of crisis, for example, or when employees are not capable of making the necessary decisions to move the organization to success.

## Participatory Leader

The participatory leader will share decision making with the team or at least seek input before making decisions regarding issues facing the organization. He or she will look for aid in creating a shared vision and develop a guiding plan with the participation of all members of the team. This leadership style results in much greater levels of employee buy-in and therefore greater chances of creative and innovative output.

## Mentor Leader

A mentor leader is someone who is an expert and shares his or her knowledge and experience to make it easier for everyone else. This leader works with others in the role of mentor to help them gain knowledge in order to improve their performance. This helps younger and newer employees to learn the ropes more quickly. It also helps develop future leaders for the organization.

**COACH LEADER PRODUCES GREATER CREATIVITY AND INNOVATION**

SMART

MANAGING

Referring to Figure 13-1, you can see that the more you behave as a coach leader, the greater the creative and innovative output will be from your group. As mentioned in Chapter 10, 50 percent of the world's engineers alive and working in the world live and work in Russia, but not nearly 50 percent of the world's innovations come from Russia. As a Russian engineer put it, "A bad system will beat a good man every time."

Many leaders may see their role as mentor leaders to help build sustainability in the organization and teach their employees what they know.

## Coach Leader

We now recognize a new type of leader, which we will name *coach leader*. This leader will partner with his or her employees in thought-provoking and creative processes that inspire the employees to maximize their personal and professional potential. The coach leader will lead from his or her belief and assessment that the employees are experts in their fields and quite capable of being creative and innovative.

From our own experience, as well as from the stories presented in this chapter, we consistently find that the coach leaders are able to elicit greater creativity and innovation from their teams than leaders using any of the other leadership styles. The behaviors that a coach leader normally exhibits parallel the dimensions of a creative and innovative environment (Chapter 10):

- Trust and openness
- Freedom
- Idea time
- Idea support
- Challenge and involvement

> ### Determining Your Leadership Style
>
> **CAUTION**
>
> If you want to determine your current leadership style, you can enlist the help of a personal coach or several trusted close friends. A coach is more likely to provide an accurate assessment. Close friends may not be willing or able to be completely frank.
>
> Do not interrogate your team members about your style. You are likely to get no information of any value. One manager at a large chemical company went from person to person on his team asking, "How is your morale today?" You can imagine the answers. He concluded (wrongly) that everything was OK despite the rumors—until a peer (who had nothing to lose) leveled with him.

- Risk taking
- Playfulness and humor
- Lack of interpersonal conflict
- Debate on the issues
- Valuing diversity of thinking styles

The coach leader knows how to encourage and how to help employees discover new solutions to problems and issues. They guide and partner with employees in *discovery*. As demonstrated in the stories of coach leaders presented in this chapter, the leader lives in curiosity and, as a result, asks powerful questions around the issue at hand to help the employees shift their awareness and see new possibilities. These leaders provide *freedom* for the employees to do their work, including *idea time* and *support*. They see the employees as experts in their field and encourage *risk taking* as learning. Again, they evoke inquiry and clarity by challenging the employees' assessments of the issues. Employees are personally deeply *challenged* and *involved* in problem solving.

Creating *trust, openness,* and *intimate relationships* also is clearly demonstrated in the stories. Coach leaders involve employees in powerful conversations and create opportunities for learning, both for employees and for themselves. They demonstrate *trust* by being able to live in ambiguity, that is, not having to know all the answers. They understand that the employee may have a different history with the issue at hand and that seeing things differently will be just as useful in problem solving.

*Communication* is extremely important to coach leaders. They focus on active listening and being present with the speaker. Mirroring, reframing, clarifying, and checking for understanding while looking for common meaning are part of their natural way of being in conversations. What is not said can also be heard. Through questions they can draw out what is not being said that they are observing. Coach leaders are capable of integrating and building on the employees' ideas. They practice speech acts such as requests, declarations, offers, promises, assertions, and assessments in order to avoid misunderstandings.

Understanding and using clear speech acts is important in our professional and personal lives to be effective. They are communication tools that seem simple but, if not used properly, can result in more difficulty from ineffective communications. Think how many times you have made a request of someone and not gotten the results you thought you requested. It may have been because you did not clearly articulate the condition of satisfaction. The sidebar provides a summary of some useful speech acts to practice.

---

**Speech acts** Tools for ensuring clarity in communications.

- *Assessments* describe how you feel and what you are thinking. They are your interpretations, judgments, values, beliefs, and preferences.     **KEY TERM**
- *Assertions* are statements for which you can provide evidence based on observation or for which there is widespread social agreement. These are the "facts."
- *Declarations* are statements about future possibilities, calling for what could be.
- *Requests* are statements that ask another for a particular item or behavior. They are calls for action and include *conditions of satisfaction*, such as time and quality of completion.
- *Promises* are agreements given to others to deliver a particular item or behavior.
- *Offers* are expressions of being willing to perform some action.

---

# Caring Creates Curiosity and Discovery

Discovery and learning are high on coach leaders' agenda for themselves and their staff. In the stories presented in this chapter, a common theme is that the coach leader, through caring, became curious and questioned the status quo and revealed some aspect of the organization or product

**SMART MANAGING**

**CARING IS CONTAGIOUS**

Recall the earlier story about Lou Holtz and his video, *Do Right*. Holtz says that players always ask the following three questions of their coaches:

- Can I trust you?
- Are you committed to excellence?
- Do you care about me?

When coach leaders truly care about both the business issues and the team members, everyone knows it and will go the extra mile when needed. Caring can easily spread throughout a team—but it must start with the team leader.

line that needed clarification or further inquiry. The coach leader then created opportunities and possibilities for employees to engage in discovery, learning, and change. Coach leaders are naturally inquisitive.

Coach leaders care about their organizations and their employees and, most of all, about making a difference and improving their world through examining possibilities. The degree to which coach leaders care is the degree of passion they display for their work. They generate conversations about what they are observing and enlist others in the caring and the conversations. Through their passion they are able to develop commitments with their employees, peers, and superiors to support and move people to action. As you read the stories in this chapter, you will see the flow of commitment in every story.

# Theory X and Theory Y and the Leadership Style Continuum

It is interesting to look at the work of Douglas McGregor at the MIT Sloan School of Management from the 1960s (*The Human Side of Enterprise,* McGraw-Hill, 1960). In this book he identified two very different ways of viewing workforce motivation that support our premise of the influence of leadership style on creativity and innovation output. McGregor said there are two beliefs at play when managing the motivation of workers. He termed these two types "Theory X" and "Theory Y."

## Theory X Managers

Managers who follow Theory X assume that employees are inherently lazy, dislike work, and will avoid working if possible. Consequently, workers need close supervision and control systems.

A Theory X manager's beliefs correlate with those of the authoritarian leader in our model (Figure 13-1). Theory X managers and authoritarian

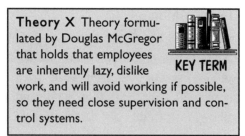

**Theory X** Theory formulated by Douglas McGregor that holds that employees are inherently lazy, dislike work, and will avoid working if possible, so they need close supervision and control systems.

**KEY TERM**

leaders kill creativity and innovation. They believe that their employees are lazy and want to avoid work because they dislike it. Further, they believe that employees must be strictly supervised and controlled in a hierarchical structure. They believe that employees have little ambition and are only interested in looking out for themselves. Therefore, the Theory X manager relies on threat and coercion to get results. This leads to an environment of mistrust, blaming, restrictions, and a lack of responsibility for the employees. There can be very little involvement, discovery, and creativity on the part of the employees. However, this result raises a big question: If an employee cared about the organization and the outcome when hired, who killed the caring?

The answer is, of course, *management*. Management sets the environment. The environment is a mirror or reflection of what managers believe and how they behave. A Theory X manager will automatically create an environment in which the employees respond as expected or they leave. This environment will not be a very creative or a fun place to work.

---

### WHO KILLED THE DEADWOOD?

**SMART**

I once attended a presentation by the famous Dr. W. Edwards Deming, an American statistician credited with improving productivity in the U.S. during WWII and in Japan after WWII. He was speaking about quality improvement in organizations and employee involvement. A man in the audience raised his hand and asked, "Dr. Deming, but what about the deadwood in the organization?" Deming replied rather forcefully and irritated, "No one wakes up in the morning to go to work to do a bad job. If he is dead, who the hell killed him?"

**MANAGING**

I agree. If the employee appears to be not trustworthy, uninvolved, without energy, resistant to change, and lazy, who created the environment that led to this negative situation?

### Theory Y Managers

On the other hand, managers who follow Theory Y assume that employees enjoy working, *may be* ambitious, may be self-motivated, and may exercise control over their work. Theory Y managers believe that most people will want to do their work well, under the right conditions, and will be motivated by the satisfaction of doing a good job.

Theory Y reflects the positive and people-oriented beliefs of coach leaders, mentor leaders, and participatory leaders. They believe that, given the right environment, most employees will seek out and accept responsibility and want to do a good job. These leaders create an environment that encourages employee involvement and opens up new possibilities for creativity. Communication is open and Theory Y leaders build trust between themselves and their teams and among their team members.

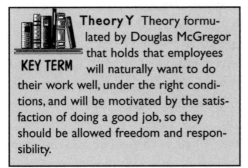

**Theory Y** Theory formulated by Douglas McGregor that holds that employees will naturally want to do their work well, under the right conditions, and will be motivated by the satisfaction of doing a good job, so they should be allowed freedom and responsibility.

On the continuum of the influence of leadership on creativity (Figure 13-1), the coach leader exemplifies the Theory Y leader. The coach leader incorporates all of the leadership traits above and beyond. The coach leader partners with his or her employees and creates an environment that is conducive to creativity and innovation.

## What About the Team Members' Perspective?

What is it like to work for an authoritarian leader, a participatory leader, mentor leader, or a coach leader? What would you need to do as an employee to help foster creativity and innovation in the different situations? Considering the traits of the four leadership styles, how would you like working for the four types of leaders and being asked to be creative? How would you like to be coached by leaders using these four styles?

You can get a good sense of the experience of employees from Figure 13-2, paying attention to the employee role under each type of leader. These roles are reflected in the stories below.

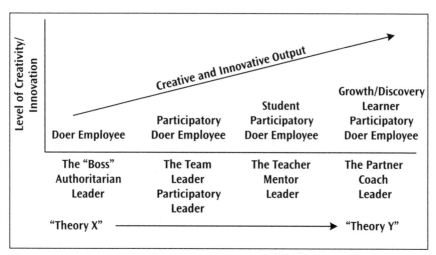

Figure 13-2. Leadership style and employee growth and discovery

## Working Under an Authoritarian Leader

If your boss were an authoritarian leader, how would approach him or her with new ideas or concerns? How do you think your ideas would be received? Chances are you would have as little contact as possible with your boss.

I was once brought into an organization by a person whom I very much liked when I knew her outside of work. This woman was my new boss. When I showed up for work, I began to notice how people got quiet when she came around and absolutely avoided her if at all possible. It turned out she was a strong authoritarian boss and ruled with an iron fist.

At the time she was in the process of building an organization development team within a large organization. She was very interested in getting acknowledgment and recognition from higher-ups.

The department began to slowly disintegrate. There was no open communication. None of us would share our concerns or our ideas for improvement with her, because we all knew she would reject both our ideas and us. As for me, working for an authoritarian leader shut me down and I worked in my own little world, avoiding her at all costs. The team was not successful and eventually failed. Think how successful we might have been if she had been a participatory leader or, better yet, a coach leader!

### Working Under a Participatory Leader

In contrast, I once worked for a participatory leader who had a staff of senior employees. This leader included his direct reports in regular meetings and encouraged discussions on the issues, including asking for recommendations. I felt valued and important and I shared my ideas freely. I even took the lead on presenting issues. I worked hard for this leader, I enjoyed it, and I would have done anything this leader asked me to do.

### Working Under a Mentor Leader

In recounting his experience working with a mentor leader, Jack said, "My experience with a mentor leader was great up to a point. After a year or so, I felt I had learned all I needed to know from him and I may even have surpassed his knowledge of getting the job done. Unfortunately, he was unwilling to move to a different relationship with me and I was stuck with being constantly mentored on how to do my job."

At first a mentor leader can be helpful and a breath of fresh air. However, as time goes by and you have learned to handle the position, if the relationship doesn't progress you can feel stuck and frustrated for not be recognized as the expert you have become.

### Working Under a Coach Leader

The best leader I have ever worked for in my career was a coach leader. She was passionate about what we were doing. She enrolled me in the cause and I was energized. It took her about a year to develop deep trusting relationships with and within her leadership team. We openly shared issues and questioned each other to discover all possibilities. We learned to include humor and playfulness in our work together. We shared openly and with pleasure so the other members would be successful. It was stimulating, energizing, and exciting and I felt valued, important, and listened to. Looking back, this was one of the highlights of my career. A coach leader will lead his or her team to surpass their goals and expectations while having a good time doing it.

## Making the Transformation to Coach Leader

Are you interested in getting results that enable you and your team to be more effective and perform better? Do you have a passion to create a team that is creative and innovative? What practices will help you behave as a coach leader and transform your organization's results? Are you willing to transform your style to be the leader of a #1 team, such as the leaders in our stories?

# Transformation at a Financial Institution

This is a story about the transformation of a participatory and sometimes authoritarian leader into a coach leader, the benefits it brought to him and to his staff, and the kinds of things he did to effect the transformation. You may find this story helpful if you, too, wish to make such a transition.

In looking for stories of successful coach leaders, I got in touch with my good friend Angela Robinson, who is Senior Vice President with one of the top 10 financial companies in the United States. She is an internal leadership coach, ICF certified, and sales management consultant. Angela is gifted at helping her clients transform into coach leaders.

She had many stories to share, but the one that left a lasting impression was of a line business manager who was promoted to regional president. For this story we will call him Mike. He was a 25-year veteran in the financial industry and a very good line business manager. He had been in a regional executive management capacity for a number of years and when he was promoted to regional president he welcomed the opportunity.

As he began transitioning into his new and prominent position, he quickly became overwhelmed with the work and responsibilities that came with being a regional president. There were more civic duties, client calls, a team to develop, and a region that needed to be well-positioned to leverage every opportunity—not to mention he had a goal of being #1 in the company based on a balanced scorecard ranking.

By disposition, as a manager he was generally open, flexible, and good at going with the flow. He managed his team leaders and relationship managers with a direct, informative approach. He got results. This style had served him as a line leader, but he was beginning to understand that this style might not serve him as well in his new role.

As a part of his transition, the company hired Angela as his coach. Mike was receptive to the idea and yet did not know how he would choose to change his behaviors to transform into a coach leader.

Mike took over his role in the fall, about two months before year-end. As the year rounded out, the region stood in the middle of the pack— ranked 11th on the company's balanced scorecard. Being mediocre was not Mike's style. At first, he approached his new team, men and women with whom he had been a peer only a few months before, with the same tell-and-direct style that had been successful in the past. It didn't seem to work as effectively and frustration set in.

After two months of working with Angela, Mike began to consider enrolling his new regional senior leadership team. He decided to begin by meeting with them in mid-January as a way to kick off the new year. After some introductory remarks, Mike stepped to a white board and wrote "11." He stated that he didn't like being 11th and it made him feel average and mediocre. Then he asked his team, "What does being 11th feel like to you?" He was curious and open and provided the opportunity for the team members to express themselves. He encouraged the conversation by asking, "Tell me, what is going on for you?"

This inquisitive behavior was new for Mike and his staff. Soon the conversation developed. It required that Mike be patient and silent, behavior unfamiliar to him. He listened intently, avoiding his desire to assess or judge what was being said.

After the team members had discussed their feelings about being #11, Mike stepped to the board and crossed out one of the 1s in "11," which left the number "1." And then he asked, "What would it be like to be #1 by the end of the year?"

The emotional space in the room opened up. The others sat straighter in their chairs as they began to envision the possibility. Mike was involving his team deeply in the challenge. (Recall from Chapter 10 that challenge and involvement are one of the dimensions for the climate for innovation).

Initially, Mike thought he did not need to change his style of leadership. He thought that his mix of authoritarian and participatory leadership styles that got him to his new position was all he needed to be successful.

Angela began her relationship with Mike by identifying what he wanted. She leveraged his desire of being ranked #1 overall on the company's balance scorecard to open him up to different ways of leading, managing, and coaching his team. They spent hours dissecting together, Angela observed Mike in action, supported him in creating a structure for managing commitments, and even gave him new distinctions that allowed him to make better decisions and communicate more effectively. They identified different moods and dispositions, as well as how he physically carried himself as #1 when he would meet with individual team members or the team as a whole. He had to define and construct what his team would look like if they were #1. He decided he needed to project being determined, resilient, steadfast, and stable.

At the end of the first six months, teammates all across the corporation began to notice a difference in how Mike was engaging; it was showing up in his results, as well. He was enrolling his direct reports in his vision through individual coaching. They were co-creating actions that started to transform the organization. They collaborated on new, innovative ways to work across business lines that set best practice standards within the company. He was helping his team see many new possibilities through their collaborative vision of being #1 and living in the question of "What might be?" and "How might we do it?" He lived in discovery with his staff in one-on-one discussions for the first few months.

> ### BEING COACHED REQUIRED A NEW MINDSET
> **TRICKS OF THE TRADE**
>
> In the beginning, Mike was unfamiliar with working with a coach, but thanks to Angela's approach, he quickly learned that the coach and he were partners in his transformation. He even included his executive assistant in his transformation by asking her to make sure that he lived the commitments that he made to himself and to others. They jointly created a workable plan for scheduling his time in meetings, for preparation, away from the office, and for weekly reflection.

All of this took practice with his coach when preparing for meetings and practice at noticing when he had slipped out of this new way of leading that was gaining such traction. Coaching was working for Mike and his coach leader style was evolving.

In March the regional rankings were announced and his region had moved up from 11th to 8th. Mike now saw the effectiveness of transforming his leadership style. He was proud of his team and freely gave them credit for their work and their commitment to being #1.

In June everything started to change. Mike moved his powerful coaching discussions from individual staff members to the team meetings. At first it was very uncomfortable to be curious, questioning, actively listening, and co-creating actions when he was used to being the authoritarian "Boss."

In July Mike's team discovered it had moved from 8th to 6th place. The corporation's most senior executive leaders even acknowledged Mike's achievements. His way of being was shifting and people began to wonder if this could really last. Mike knew he needed to sustain this new energy and style. He was morphing physically into a new type of leader. His dispositions became less awkward; the practice was taking hold and becoming more natural. The time and effort he and his coach had invested are paying off in more ways than simply moving up in ranking.

In October his region came in 3rd. In January of the following year, at the corporation's annual sales leadership conference, Mike learned his region achieved 2nd place! They had gone from 11th to 2nd out of 20 in approximately 10 months.

This was a direct result of his personal transformation from authoritarian leader to coach leader. He was able to recruit others into his vision of being #1 and shift how he worked with them as their leader and coached them to become different leaders as well.

His shift in leadership style brought the following results for this region:

**SMART MANAGING**

### WORKING TWO LEADERSHIP STYLES

Mike's team rose from 11th to 2nd place (out of 20) in just 10 months. This was a direct result of his personal transformation from authoritarian leader to coach leader. This is yet another confirmation of the validity of the leadership continuum (Figure 13-1), which shows that performance (creative and innovative output) will improve as a leader transitions toward the coach leader end of the continuum. Mike had not abandoned his ability to behave in the authoritarian style when it might be appropriate, but he had added the ability to behave in the coach leader style when he needed greater creative and innovative results.

- They reorganized their structure.
- They improved processes.
- They created teaming at the grassroots level.
- They developed partnering across their departments.
- They developed clear lines of communication for the bank's clients as soon as they walked through the door.
- Clients perceived their experience in new and friendlier ways.

Mike had become a coach leader and had learned how to move from one style of leadership to another, as shown in Figure 13-1, as appropriate for the situation. He learned how to enroll his staff. He asked his staff questions and got them living in the question of wondering what could be different. He gave his staff permission to live in discovery and growth.

# Practices for Transforming to a Coach Leader

Use these practices to help you transition your leader style to the next level.

If you are now an *authoritarian leader*, to move to the next level you could:

- Start by holding regularly scheduled team meetings.
- Share what you are working on and what is going on at your level and above.
- Ask team members to share what they are working on.
- Have in-depth conversations with your team about all issues that affect them and their staff.
- When possible, ask the team for input on decisions you are making.

If you are now a *participative leader*, to move to the next level you could:

- Continue the practices listed above.
- Create a learning environment: create a learning plan for each team member.
- Ask each member of your team where he or she wants to be in three to five years.
- Take time in your team meetings for learning moments to educate or train your team so they can progress.

- Share your expertise and experience.
- Bring in outside experts.
- Share with your team what you know about an issue.
- Ask team members to share their knowledge.
- Ask team members to participate in decisions that affect them.

If you are now a *mentor leader*, to move to the next level you could:

- Continue the practices listed above.
- Practice engaging in purposeful and powerful conversations about issues affecting the team.
- Share issues you are passionate about and enroll team members.
- Build trust by being vulnerable and sharing stories of times when you tried new things and failed. Share the learning.
- Ask the team members to share similar stories.
- In your powerful conversations, lead the team members in discovery by asking questions. Be curious. Drill down to the bottom to find understanding of the issues. Don't be the expert; let them be in discovery.
- Practice active listening. Mirror back for understanding. Be in an open body position.
- Practice being aware of when you are judging or assessing and check your assessments.
- Practice examining your temperament. Where do you need to be to create a creative team?
  - resolution and commitment
  - stability and order

---

**TRICKS OF THE TRADE**

### OPEN BODY POSITION

Being in an *open body position* means your arms and legs are not crossed and your hands are flat, not closed. That's part of showing you are listening with interest and an open mind.

Face the other person fully. If standing, move slightly closer to the other person. If seated, lean forward slightly.

Make eye contact but don't stare. While listening, occasionally nod if you're in agreement.

Notice how you stand or sit while talking with people and how you position your hands and legs. It may help to practice in front of a mirror, so you know how others perceive your body language.

- flexibility and boldness
- openness and enrolling

■ Practice guiding the team in conversations that open up the members' awareness to see new, unexpected, and useful possibilities.

■ Practice living in the question, "What could be different?" Share that question with the team.

Congratulations! You are coach leader! You have arrived! You are fostering creativity and innovation in your team members!

# Demonstrating Caring Led to Breakthroughs
## Sustained Fund Raising at American Red Cross

Kathleen Loehr served as interim Senior Vice President of Development for the American Red Cross National Headquarters from 2005 to 2008. As a result of her previous five years at the Red Cross within the Development department, Kathleen knew that the current fundraising model was not sustainable. Direct mail revenue was declining. Donors were not renewing. Many donors contributed only once, such as for a major disaster like Katrina. Donors were giving annual gifts that were eight times more generous to other nonprofits than to the Red Cross. There was no ability to track or analyze donor behavior, as the headquarters and the 700-plus chapters did not share a database.

Even before Kathleen assumed the role of interim Senior Vice President, she had a vision of a sustainable fundraising model that focused on the donors and was built on trust and collaboration between headquarters and the chapters. Now that she was in a position of influence she began the initiative to create a sustainable fundraising process.

For her initiative to work, Kathleen needed the cooperation of the Board of Directors, senior leaders, the individual chapters, and headquarters development staff. This was particularly challenging because the chapters historically found no value in cooperating and collaborating with headquarters since they retained their individual fund-raising results to support their individual chapter. You might even say they viewed themselves as competing with headquarters.

In December 2005, the Board of Directors charged Red Cross management to develop a comprehensive, long-term plan to improve

**SMART**

**MANAGING**

## BUILD TRUST THROUGH UNBRIDLED OPENNESS

Kathleen Loehr was the coach leader throughout this process, both in her attitude and in her behavior. The major issue she needed to overcome was the basic distrust between the chapters and headquarters. Her role as coach leader of this initiative was to build relationships, build trust through openness, and get agreement on the desired outcome. In this role she presented her vision to the Board and leaders at national headquarters and in chapters.

Kathleen began powerful conversations about what this initiative might look like when implemented. She built a project leadership team that also used the same philosophy of opening up the conversation through powerful questioning. She and her team built trust, openness, intimacy, and agreement between the chapters and headquarters to begin discussions about a new way of fundraising *together*. This was a major milestone, since they had never before worked to cooperate regarding fundraising using shared vision, goals, and principles.

fundraising across the entire organization. Kathleen immediately built a talented core leadership team to focus on the newly named Strategic Fundraising Initiative (SFI). This project team created and tested goals, assumptions, and a framework for a plan through May 2006. At that time, the Board accepted the conceptual plan and the SFI was formally launched. A vision statement was created by September 2006 and tested across all chapters in the field with conference calls and meetings. Shortly thereafter, an SFI Advisory Board made up of 11 chapter leaders and volunteers was established to provide high-level direction and guidance to the SFI project team. Through fall 2006 and winter 2007, over 40 individuals within national headquarters and in chapters collaborated to assess the current state, design the future state and the specific business plan, and create the detailed implementation plan.

In the role of coach leader, Kathleen was able to stay neutral in the process. She did not set herself up as an authority on the team (authoritarian leader), as a team leader who only asked for input in decision-making (participatory leader), or as a teacher (mentor leader). She clearly was operating from the coach leader position shown in Figure 13-1. She consistently expressed curiosity by asking many open-ended questions and helped participants live in the uncomfortable place of uncertainty, which facilitated thinking "out of the box" to find unexpected solutions.

For example, they conducted a survey of over 2,000 Red Cross donors to understand how they gave and what might increase their giving. They used a consultant to create workshops that were highly participatory and deftly facilitated so that more than 40 individuals could do their best thinking in three days on a new design for working with millions of donors across the Red Cross system. From these two inputs, they created a standardized process tailored to the type of donor based on how the donor first gave—whether in response to a disaster, through general direct mail, or through a personal solicitation.

This new approach alerted the entire organization that a commitment to donor relationships was the key to increasing revenue and ensuring long-term fundraising success. Acting as a coach leader, Kathleen and the team created a sustainable and collaborative fundraising model between the chapters and headquarters, achieving a first in the history of the American Red Cross.

Kathleen left upon completion of the initiative's detailed design, which included metrics, funding requirements, and implementation steps. The core principles and design rules held true with the change of leadership at the Board and management levels and the Red Cross is now implementing its first-ever shared database, centralized direct mail, and donor-focused solicitation that is collaborative across the system. This new foundation of strategic fund-raising has allowed the Red Cross to meet its fund-raising goals and engage more long-term donors. Kathleen's vision became reality as a result of her coach leader behavior and style.

## $5 Million Savings at Ingersoll Rand

Larry Burnette was the Director of Compensation at Ingersoll Rand from September 2001 to February 2007. Prior to moving to Ingersoll Rand, he was a leader in HR at DuPont with a staff of 85

> ### Build Trust by Adopting the Coach Leader Style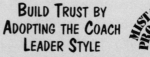
>
> A lack of trust prevented any collaboration between chapters and headquarters in fundraising. Donors were considered "owned" by either headquarters or one of the chapters, but never both. Also, there was no overarching vision for improving the fundraising process.
>
> Kathleen built trust by using the coach leader style.

employees. In that position he had led his staff as a coach leader to be innovative in shifting their perception of being only a service provider to DuPont to one of expanding services to new markets.

When Larry arrived at Ingersoll Rand, he assessed that everything was in a state of disarray and the staff was underused. Larry said, "The previous director was on a power trip. I realized that, in order to create change and allow creativity and innovation to flourish, I had to create an environment based on trust and mutual respect. Setting the right environment was critical to improving performance."

First, Larry let his staff know that he was there to support them and that he knew they were the experts. He purposefully remained calm in crises and avoided irrational behavior as he learned about the organization and the compensation system, which he felt was in great need of improvement. From his experience as a coach leader at DuPont, Larry knew that his behaviors would help him to transform his organization. He built trust by empowering his people to make decisions and by being open and honest with them. He wanted them to bring him solutions, instead of just bringing problems and asking his direction, as his predecessor would likely have done. He asked open-ended questions like "What do you think we should do?", "If we did that what would be the result?", and "What other options have you considered?" He took time to listen and to help his people see that they had the answers and that they were experts in their field. It was exciting work to watch his staff members come into their own.

At one point in his learning, Larry realized that the company was paying inordinately high taxes and tax penalties. He started asking questions about this situation, but his staff could offer little explanation. Larry then asked one of the tax attorneys, an intimidating sort of person. He discovered that the tax attorney had no answers either. He then began probing the corporate tax attorneys with his questions. They gave him large boxes full of documents to discourage his inquiry, but did not provide any answers. Not satisfied with the status quo and having identified a major issue, Larry continued to seek answers. Finally realizing that Larry wasn't going to go away quietly and that this issue was indeed important, the tax attorneys agreed to collaborate and work with the HR staff to resolve this issue.

Having identified a major issue with his staff through powerful questions and discovery, he formed a team for discovery. Larry's passion for fixing the problem was apparent and his deep caring helped everyone to participate fully on his team.

Their focus was to discover the origin of these tax fees and penalties and to find

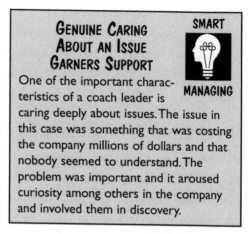

**GENUINE CARING ABOUT AN ISSUE GARNERS SUPPORT**

SMART

MANAGING

One of the important characteristics of a coach leader is caring deeply about issues. The issue in this case was something that was costing the company millions of dollars and that nobody seemed to understand. The problem was important and it aroused curiosity among others in the company and involved them in discovery.

out how they could be stopped. The team consisted of members of the compensation office and the tax attorney's office, who agreed to work together as a result of the relationships Larry had built.

What they discovered was that Ingersoll consisted of 35-plus legal entities, each with its own payroll tax ID. When employees were moved between companies, Ingersoll ended up paying more taxes. Penalties were incurred due to the sheer complexity of the long-standing structure that no one had previously questioned.

The team recommended collapsing the 35-plus companies' tax IDs into one company, which would be a holding company for all employees for payroll purposes. The team presented this solution to headquarters and it was approved. This whole process took approximately two years to accomplish and Ingersoll Rand saved approximately $5 million a year on payroll and state unemployment taxes.

As a coach leader, Larry had identified a major issue through powerful questions to his staff. He then empowered a team to do discovery on the issue and make recommendations on solutions. He saw his role as asking powerful questions and giving his team members the time, support, and freedom to do their research to develop a better practice. He encouraged them to seek internal data as well as external data. He supported their professional development in attending conferences and getting training.

Larry showed his coach leader style by being a visionary, deeply caring about the issue, building trust, involving his employees in powerful conversations, communicating effectively, helping team members identify major blocks to being more effective, providing freedom and time and support to develop solutions, encouraging learning and discovery, building relationships and collaboration, and encouraging his staff to live in discovery.

## Breakthrough Products at a Major U.S. Corporation

In 2000, a new management team was installed at a large producer of polyurethane foam products. The products were mostly for slow-growth commodity markets, including furniture, bedding, and industrial applications such as packaging. These products were under price pressure and yet costs continued to rise. In this difficult situation, the challenge facing this new management team was to identify growth opportunities with innovative new products that would be compatible with the company's core manufacturing and product lines.

A business development group was established, reporting directly to the CEO level. This organizational feature alone helped shield this new group from day-to-day pressures, allowing it to be more innovative. The new vice president of this group, Richard ("Dick") Good, was highly experienced and trained in business development and product development.

His management style was truly to act as an enabling coach leader. Dick said, "I look for people who have an inclination for business development, that is, those who have high tolerance for uncertainty, and among those I want the ones who don't mind taking a risk to bend a few of the organizational rules. Then I give them the freedom to pursue their own goals in an atmosphere that helps them 'look beyond the box' as they do their work. I see myself as coach leader for the team using my background and experience."

### New Bedding Product

The team assigned to the bedding market identified a need to improve performance of the cushioning material used in quilt top mattresses. The fiber cushioning was deficient in durability and would collapse after a short time of use. The team was successful in developing a new polyurethane foam that provided the soft comfort of fiber and the durability of polyurethane. Even more important, it was based on a core manufacturing process that was proprietary, which gave the company a competitive advantage in the marketplace. A new brand was established, resulting in a highly successful new product line that could be leveraged to carry the other commodity cushioning products.

## New Packaging Foam Product

In another opportunity, the team assigned to the packaging market headed by Michael Hnatow identified a need for higher performance at lower weight. A new, lightweight packaging foam was developed, using a proprietary core manufacturing process, and a new brand was established.

However, a major organizational issue threatened the economic success of this new product: the salespeople were paid commissions based on product price, and this was a lower-priced product. Dick Good, Michael's leader, coached Michael, who realized that the foam industry needed a new design model and reasons to adopt this new packaging foam. Michael created the new model that convinced the trade, and Dick resolved the sales commission issue, which removed this barrier. Customers responded immediately and positively.

## Children's Furniture Product

As an example of unusual behavior supported by Dick, one of the teams decided to use an outside innovation consulting company to facilitate innovative problem solving. This was a dramatic departure from previous approaches to business growth and new product development—and the business results were impressive.

The issue was how to innovate in solid foam core children's furniture. This was one of the most challenging areas, since these products were historically sold at low margin to retail merchandisers such as Walmart.

Michael Hnatow, project manager, explained that after this team completed a workshop using pattern-breaking thinking (see Chapter 8), some new and novel approaches were identified. Two areas were selected to pursue. One option was a direct sale to the consumer via the Internet; the other approach identified an opportunity for direct sale to the children's day care industry. Both of these new market directions provided a much more profitable channel to market than the traditional low-margin retail outlets. Dick Good's coach leader behavior was to give his organization freedom and support in taking the highly unusual approach of using an innovation consulting company to help identify ways to improve the business.

## Making Connections Yields Big Results in Radically New Product

Perhaps the most radical new product innovation that occurred related to micro fuel cells. The jump from furniture cushioning to the high-tech sector of micro fuel cells was a giant leap that was supported by Dick as coach leader, who again gave his organization the freedom to live in discovery.

It all began when Dr. Mark Kinkelaar, director of business development for technical products, attended an energy conference and learned of a problem for micro fuel cells that were in early development stage at that time. Various companies were working to introduce micro fuel cells as high-energy, portable power to replace batteries in portable devices such as computers, music players, and cell phones. The fuel cell needed to perform under all conditions—up, down, or sideways; otherwise, disruptions would occur in electrical power.

Mark Kinkelaar made the connection between the need and a proprietary polyurethane foam wicking material that was currently used in ink-

---

**SMART**

**MANAGING**

### How Breakthroughs Happen

These kinds of connections are described beautifully in Andrew Hargadon's book, *How Breakthroughs Happen* (Harvard Business School Press, 2003). Hargadon points out that we are more likely to make productive connections with people with whom we have weak ties (our secondary networks) rather than people with whom we have strong ties (our primary networks) since we tend to know more what each other knows. This is one of the chief reasons it's a good idea to send your people to conferences and meetings so that connections can be made, as Mark Kinkelaar did in the micro fuel cell story. Some managers even encourage employees to attend one conference per year *outside* their immediate work area just to increase the chances of making such connections. In the fishing lure story (Chapter 10), Phil Harman was given the freedom and the resources to attend a fishing show in Las Vegas to promote his new fishing lure and to get new ideas.

> ### Vested Interest in Old Technology Opposes New Technology
>
> This exciting and highly creative micro fuel cell development was not without its organizational problems. A highly successful specialty foam was being used in nickel metal hydride (NiMH) batteries, a market that was rapidly declining because it was moving off-shore. When Kinkelaar presented his new fuel cell foam product idea, it was vigorously opposed by the executive vice president, who was relying on the NiMH product for much-needed profits. He was so aligned with supporting his current business that he failed to see the market was moving away from NiMH technology and he was not prepared to embrace new opportunities.
>
> This is an excellent example of how authoritarian leadership diminishes innovation. Which kind of leader would you rather be—authoritarian leader or coach leader?

jet printer cartridges to ensure a continuous and smooth supply of ink. He reasoned correctly that the same type of foam could provide continuous power in micro fuel cells that used alcohol as the fuel.

This idea led to patents for a disposable cartridge lined with the foam wicking material. With further development, the idea led to plans for an IPO to spin off a new company to manufacture the micro fuel cell cartridges! Mark was working in an environment that was characterized by trust, freedom, and the encouragement to continuously look for new opportunities and new connections.

The foregoing are some good examples of the kinds of results that can occur in a new product/business development activity when people are free to reach beyond existing paradigms and preconceived beliefs and discover new business opportunities with a coach leader management style. Dick Good said, "It is very clear to me that the coach leader style of management was crucial to the high level of innovative output that we achieved. Less experienced and less informed managers who use an authoritarian style would have been far less successful in leading their teams to innovative outcomes."

## Leader Coaches Involve People All the Way

When thinking of leaders who are coaches of innovation, one who immediately comes to mind is Rebecca Locke. Rebecca is currently

**SMART MANAGING**

### COACH LEADERS FOSTER CREATIVITY

One of the major lessons here is that the truth of Figure 13-1 is continually confirmed in story after story. For managers who want to foster creativity and innovation in teams, the message is clear: learning to be an effective coach leader is an important step.

Director of the Division of Planned Giving in Development at the American Red Cross National Headquarters in Washington, DC.

Over the last several years, the American Red Cross National Headquarters has been in a state of chaos and flux characterized by constant reorganizations, changes in leadership, and lack of funds. However, during that time, due to Rebecca's great leadership skills, her division has grown to a staff of 43 people. As her staff has grown, the old expectation that frontline managers serve as both managers and fundraisers was just not a workable situation, because managers were spreading themselves too thin to continue to be successful. She understood that a drastic change was needed in the way her group was organized. She also understood that, as a result of the chaos of the last several years, people were resistant to change and upset by it.

Rebecca challenged her staff of 43 to work on developing a new structure. Rebecca understood that behaving as a coach leader would allow her to facilitate learning and help employees discover for themselves solutions to the important issue of reorganization. She also understood there would likely be resistance from the staff if she decided on the reorganization and just told them how it would be.

She understood that adopting coaching behavior as the leader could facilitate learning and help the staff welcome whatever structure they might develop. The tools of coaching she used were to have powerful conversations and powerful questions and to engage in active listening to coach the staff to create a new structure for her organization.

The staff began by looking at the processes and tracking its work. They put together a model structure that would have required adding new positions, which they proposed to Rebecca. They found out that the funding was not immediately available for the new positions, which included four full-time managers who did not also have to do fundraising. Rebecca then coached the team to develop creative ways of implementing its ideas until funding might become available.

As a result, the team developed a way to implement 70 percent of its ideas without an increase in funding. The team presented its solution to Rebecca and she presented it to her Senior Vice President.

In the debriefing the Senior VP asked Rebecca when she was going to tell her staff about the restructuring. Rebecca replied that she didn't need to tell them, since they had developed this new plan themselves and they were all on board with it! Each team member knew where and how he or she would fit into the new organization since they each had identified which roles they wanted to play and which jobs they wanted to have. (By the way, funding for full implementation was soon found, allowing a more productive fund-raising effort.)

When I asked Rebecca why she had managed the reorganization in this way, she stated that it would have been out of character to do any other way. She said, "I have built a team of exceptionally talented people and I want to retain them because they are happy and involved. If any of my people resign for a better job, I want there to at least be a $10,000 increase in salary before they would even consider leaving."

Rebecca is an exemplary leader who uses coaching to yield innovative solutions to important problems confronting the organization. She truly sees her role as a leader coach to help her team members see different possibilities and to build its futures in the organization.

# Manager's Checklist for Chapter 13

☑ Enlist the help of a personal coach or several trusted close friends to help you determine your current predominant management style. You will probably get the most accurate answer from a coach. Close friends may not be willing or able to be completely frank.

☑ If you currently prefer the authoritarian style and decide to move toward the coach leader style, begin by taking small steps as outlined in the sections, "Four Leadership Styles for Creativity and Innovation" and "Making the Transformation to Coach Leader."

☑ As you become more open and share more information with your team members, they will begin sharing more information with you.

(Review Chapter 10 on the relationship between openness and trust.) This is the beginning of building greater trust. Don't expect it to happen overnight.

☑ Caution: Do not interrogate your team members about your style. You are likely to get no information of any value.

☑ Have fun as you move toward being a manager who truly fosters creativity and innovation in your team.

**About the author of this chapter:** Jack Johnson owns his own Executive Coaching practice helping executives at all levels dramatically improve performance. He is formerly Senior Organization Development Consultant and Executive Coach for the American Red Cross and formerly internal Organization Development Consultant and Executive Coach for The Smithsonian Institution. He earned the title of Certified Professional Coach from the International Coach Federation, and holds a Certificate of Organization Development from Georgetown University, and a Certificate of Organizational Creativity and Innovation from Innovation University of which he is a Founding Fellow.

Jack is a registered architect and previously served as such for the Navy, Army, and Air Force Corps of Engineers, as well as private industry. He holds a Bachelor's and Master's Degree of Architecture, and a graduate level Certificate in Engineering Administration. He can be reached at www.coachjackjohnson.com.

Appendix

# Worksheets

## Worksheet #1. Clarifying Benefits

Benefit #1 _____

_____

_____

Benefit #2 _____

_____

_____

Benefit #3 _____

_____

_____

Benefit #4 _____

_____

_____

Benefit #5 _____

_____

_____

## Worsheet #2. Overcoming Concerns

| Concerns About the Idea | Actions to Overcome Concerns |
|---|---|
| #1 _____ | #1 _____ |
| #2 _____ | #2 _____ |
| #3 _____ | #3 _____ |
| #4 _____ | #4 _____ |
| #5 _____ | #5 _____ |

## Worksheet #3. Identify Critical Tests

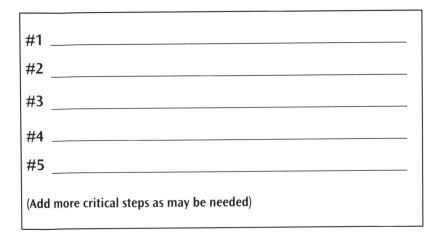

#1 _____

#2 _____

#3 _____

#4 _____

#5 _____

(Add more critical steps as may be needed)

## Worksheet #4. Tree Diagram

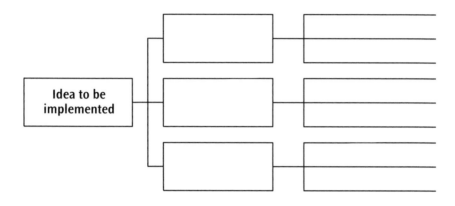

## Worksheet #5. Who Will Do What by When?

|  | Month 1 | Month 2 | Month 3 | Month 4 | Month 5 | Month 6 | Month 7 |
|---|---|---|---|---|---|---|---|
| Action 1 |  |  |  |  |  |  |  |
| Action 2 |  |  |  |  |  |  |  |
| Action 3 |  |  |  |  |  |  |  |
| Action 4 |  |  |  |  |  |  |  |

# Index

# About the Author

**Charles (Charlie) Prather** is president of Bottom Line Innovation Associates, Inc., helping organizations develop innovation as a core competency. Many of the Fortune 100 companies are clients, representing chemicals, paper, consumer products, high-tech, government, financial services, and other segments.

Charlie served DuPont some 24 years in numerous R&D and leadership positions. He was appointed Manager of the DuPont Center for Creativity and Innovation upon its formation and helped shape its direction and design its offerings. Charlie earned his Ph.D. in biochemistry from North Carolina State University. He is Senior Fellow of the Robert H. Smith School of Business at the University of Maryland, College Park.

Charlie is a frequent keynote speaker and conference presenter. He has published many articles; the most recent are listed below. His first book, *Blueprints for Innovation*, was published by American Management Association (1995). He can be reached at Charlie@BottomLineInnovation.com or 800-220-9375 inside the USA or +1-954-480-7607 outside the USA. His Web site is *www.bottomlineinnovation.com*.

Some recent publications:

- "Keeping Innovation Alive After the Consultants Leave," *Research-Technology Management*, Vol. 43, No. 5, September-October 2000.
- "Involve Everyone in the Innovation Process," *Research-Technology Management*, Vol. 45, No. 5, September-October 2002.
- "Enhancing Organizational Knowledge Creation for Breakthrough Innovation: Tools and Techniques" (with Peter Koen, Richard McDermott, and Robb Olsen), Chapter 4 in *PDMA Toolbook 2 for New Product Development* (Hoboken, NJ: John Wiley & Sons, 2004).
- "The Dumb Thing About SMART Goals for Innovation," *Research-Technology Management*, Vol. 48, No. 5, September-October 2005.
- "Use Mistakes to Foster Innovation," *Research-Technology Management*, Vol. 51, No. 2, March-April 2008.